GRAPHICS PROGRAMMING POWERPACK

Michael Jones

SAMS
PUBLISHING

A Division of Prentice Hall Computer Publishing
11711 North College, Carmel, Indiana 46032 USA

PUBLISHER
Richard K. Swadley

ACQUISITIONS MANAGER
Jordan Gold

ACQUISITIONS EDITOR
Gregory Croy

DEVELOPMENT EDITOR
Stacy Hiquet

PRODUCTION EDITOR
Fran Hatton

EDITORS
Michael Cunningham
Sandy Doell
Grant Fairchild
Melba Hopper
Dean Miller

EDITORIAL COORDINATORS
Rebecca S. Freeman
Bill Whitmer

EDITORIAL ASSISTANTS
Rosemarie Graham
Lori Kelley

TECHNICAL EDITOR
Tim Moore

COVER DESIGNER
Jean Bisesi

**DIRECTOR OF PRODUCTION
AND MANUFACTURING**
Jeff Valler

PRODUCTION MANAGER
Corinne Walls

IMPRINT MANAGER
Matthew Morrill

BOOK DESIGNER
Michele Laseau

PRODUCTION ANALYST
Mary Beth Wakefield

**PROOFREADING/INDEXING
COORDINATOR**
Joelynn Gifford

INDEXER
Sherry Massey

PRODUCTION
Terri Edwards
Dennis Clay Hager
John Kane
R. Sean Medlock
Michelle Self
Susan Shepard
Greg Simsic
Angie Trzepacz
Alyssa Yesh

OVERVIEW

TABLE OF
CONTENTS

ACKNOWLEDGMENTS

Thanks to Rachel, David, Aaron, Martha, and especially my wife, Sarah, for everything; and thanks to Bob Zigon for nothing.

ABOUT THE AUTHOR

Michael Jones resides in Indianapolis, Indiana, along with his wife, Sarah. He is a software engineer for Truevision, Inc., a company that specializes in developing videographic hardware and software.

INTRODUCTION

USING THE GRAPHICS POWERPACK

This section describes the contents of the Graphics PowerPack diskette and how to access PowerPack routines from your Microsoft C applications. PowerPack is designed for use with Microsoft C 5.0 or higher and DOS 2.1 or higher.

INTRODUCTION TO POWERPACK

The Graphics PowerPack is a subset of the GX Development Series by Genus Microprogramming, Inc. The GX Development Series is an extremely powerful, flexible, yet easy-to-use graphics toolkit package, hand coded and optimized in assembly language for maximum speed. The GX Development Series comes in six separate packages, which are available individually or in any combination. The Graphics PowerPack was created by selecting the most useful routines from the GX Development Series toolkit packages, and putting them together in one toolkit included with this book. If you find the Graphics PowerPack improves your productivity and makes graphics programming more fun, information about how to purchase the entire GX Developement Series at a significant discount is available in the back of the book.

The PowerPack consists of a DOS Link Library and sample source code. The library is actually several library files constructed for use in small, medium, and large memory models. The aim of this library is to accelerate and simplify graphics application building under DOS. Using the PowerPack library routines, developers can minimize programming overhead and begin building applications far sooner than if they were to develop the functionality themselves. Developers who are new to graphics programming under DOS will find that PowerPack drastically reduces their normal learning curve, enabling them to be productive in a fraction of the usual time.

PowerPack functions are designed so that you can understand the purpose of a function just by knowing the name of that function. The naming scheme is in the form [id][FunctionName]. For example, the function gxVirtualDisplay represents a graphics kernel function ID (gx) that moves data from a virtual buffer to the display. The other ID values are gr (graphics routines), fx (effects routines), and pcx (PCX image file routines).

All functions in the PowerPack are declared with the FAR PASCAL prototype definition. The FAR declaration requires that both a segment and an offset be pushed on the stack during function call operations, and is required even when working in the small memory model. The PASCAL keyword simply informs the compiler which method to use when pushing and popping stack parameters. This results in faster execution of functions. This functionality is completely invisible to the graphics programmer; it doesn't require that you change the way you write your programs.

The Graphics PowerPack is separated into four distinct graphics groups. Each group contains a unique header file and link library for small, medium, and large memory models. The following list is a detailed description of these groups.

1. **Kernel**: The kernel provides the very basic graphics functionality and is the heart of the PowerPack. The kernel contains basic functions such as gxSetMode (set the current display mode) and gxClearDisplay (clear a display page). Kernel function names always include the two-character prefix gx. The kernel is made up of the gxLib.h header file and the GX_CS.LIB small model library. In order to use any PowerPack function, you must include these files in your source code and link list.

2. **Graphics Routines**: The graphics routines are a supplement to the kernel, providing the vast majority of graphics operations such as grSetFillPattern (select a fill pattern) and grDrawRect (draw a rectangle). Graphics routines function names are distinguished by the two-character prefix gr. The graphics routines consist of the grLib.h header file and the GR_CS.LIB small model library. You must include these two files in your source code and link list to use any graphics functions that start with gr.

3. **Effects Routines**: The effects routines contain functions specific to special effects, such as fxPlaySong (play a string of notes) and fxPlayTone (play a frequency tone). All effects function names are prefixed with the two-character identifier fx. The effects routines are composed of the fxlib.h header file and the FX_CS.LIB small model library. You must include these two files in your source code and link list to use any effects functions.

4. **PCX Routines**: The PCX routines contain functions that allow the display of PCX files such as pcxVerifyFile (verify if valid PCX file) and pcxFileImage (load PCX file into memory). All PCX function names contain the three-character identifier pcx preceding the actual function name. The PCX routines are made up of the pcxlib.h header file and the PCX_CS.LIB small model library. You must include these two files in your source code and link list to use any functions that start with pcx.

With the exception of the routines that return the current drawing color or some other singular piece of requested information, PowerPack routines always return a valid return code or, when an error is encountered, an error code. Those functions that return a success or failure code return the constant gxSUCCESS for a successful operation. In case of an error, the error code returned is always negative and is a unique identifier of the problem encountered. An example follows:

```
int retValue;

retValue = gxVirtualDisplay(...);
if(retValue < 0) print_error();

/* or */

if(retValue != gxSUCCESS) print_error();
```

See Appendix A for a complete listing of valid error codes.

THE POWERPACK DISKETTE

The Graphics PowerPack libraries, include files, and examples are provided on a disk included with this book. As an extra bonus, the disk provides a full-featured game written using the PowerPack, including the source code.

To install the PowerPack on your computer system, place the PowerPack disk in drive A: and enter the following two lines (if you are installing from another drive, substitute that letter for the A:):

```
A:
INSTALL
```

Follow the menu options for installing various parts of the PowerPack, using the directories you wish. All programs and files are verified for data integrity, to ensure nothing is lost in the installation process. No modifications are performed on your environment (that is, your AUTOEXEC.BAT and CONFIG.SYS files). Note that you can run the installation program more than once, if you later wish to install parts of the PowerPack you decide to skip now.

USING THE POWERPACK IN AN APPLICATION

Very few steps are required for you to get started using PowerPack; you must perform these steps, however, if the PowerPack is to work properly—failure to do so causes unexpected results.

- You must include the appropriate header file for each of your source files that make PowerPack subroutine calls. These are the gxlib.h, grlib.h, fxlib.h, and pcxlib.h header files described earlier. These files contain the function prototypes, data structure definitions, error codes, and other information required by PowerPack. If you add the path containing the PowerPack header files to your INCLUDE environment variable, as in:

```
set INCLUDE=C:\C600\INCLUDE;C:\GENUS\INCLUDE;
```

then you simply add the following lines to your source code:

```
#include <gxlib.h>
#include <grlib.h>
```

Otherwise, you must explicitly list the pathname that contains the header files:

```
#include "c:/genus/include/gxlib.h"
#include "c:/genus/include/grlib.h"
```

The example shown references only the kernel and graphics routines. To include all functions contained in the PowerPack, you need to also include the header files fxlib.h and pcxlib.h.

- The PowerPack library files must be placed in a directory path the compiler can locate. The easiest way to accomplish this is to add to your LIB environment variable the pathname that contains the library files, as shown in the following example:

```
set LIB=C:\C600\LIB;C:\GENUS\LIB
```

- You must add the names of the PowerPack library files for which you make subroutine calls to the list of external libraries during the link procedure of the program build. For small model programs, the names of the libraries are GX_CS.LIB, GR_CS.LIB, FX_CS.LIB, and PCX_CS.LIB. The CS in the library name stands for Microsoft (or equivalent) C, small memory model. The medium model libraries are named the same, with the CS replaced by CM; large model libraries replace the CS with CL. If you don't know how to link external libraries to your program, see the example below. You should consult the manual supplied with your programming language for additional information.

- You must call the PowerPack function gxSetDisplay before calling any other PowerPack subroutine. This doesn't change the current display mode—it simply initializes the internal data structures for future subroutine calls. When you want to actually change the current display mode for graphics operations, you call the function gxSetMode.

- The following command can then be used to compile and link your programs. This example compiles and links the Apples&Oranges game, A&O, provided with the PowerPack, using the large memory model:

```
cl /AL A&O.c /link gx_cl fx_cl pcx_cl gr_cl
```

The example programs provided with the book can be compiled and linked in the same manner.

TERMINOLOGY

You must understand the terms used in this book before you can efficiently create graphics applications. Many of these terms are described in this section. This is not meant to be a complete discussion of these terms, but a brief overview.

- A *pixel* is basically a single dot of an image displayed on your screen. Sometimes it is called a *pel* (for picture element), but in this book it is called a pixel. A pixel doesn't necessarily mean a specific amount of memory in bytes; it represents a single dot among the many hundreds or thousands of dots that compose an image. For example, a single pixel in a 16-color graphics video mode takes up one half-byte of memory, whereas a pixel in a 256-color graphics video mode requires a whole byte of memory. Because PowerPack creates virtual buffers for storage of your graphics, you don't need to concentrate on calculating memory needs based on pixel requirements—PowerPack does it for you.

- *Pixel depth* is a term relating to the amount of memory devoted to displaying one pixel. The pixel depth value specifies the number of bits (not bytes) needed to display the pixel. Another name for pixel depth is *bits per pixel.* Pixel depth is determined by the display mode you choose. For example, video mode gx_VGA12 has a pixel depth of four. A pixel depth of four (four bits per pixel) computes to 2^4 colors or 16 colors. Video mode gx_VGA11, however, has a pixel depth of one (one bit per pixel), which translates to 2^1 colors or 2 colors.

- A *Color Palette* is a memory location where the values that represent the displayable colors are stored. The system actually contains two color palettes. The first stores 16 colors plus one border (overscan) color. To access a color, you reference it using the index, which ranges from 0 to 15 (not including the border color). At each index value is a number that represents a real color to be displayed. This number ranges from 0 to 63. Therefore, when you display palette color 0, you are displaying the specific color stored at index 0. The second palette stores 256 colors—the colors for the 256 color display modes. This palette also uses an index, which ranges from 0 to 255. However, each color index points to three color component values: a red color component, a green color component, and a blue color component. Each component can range from 0 to 63, giving you 262,144 colors to choose from for each of the 256 palette indexes.

- *Conventional Memory* is the memory up to 640K. All IBM-compatible personal computers have at least 256K of conventional memory. DOS resides in conventional memory, as do device drivers, terminate-and-stay-resident (TSR) utilities, and most DOS applications. In addition, PCs that contain the 80286, 80386, or 80486 CPU can have an additional 384K of memory, giving a total of 1M. This memory area usually contains programs such as the VGA BIOS and Hard Disk controller. There are memory management utilities (as well as DOS 5.0) that allow you to load ordinary programs into memory between 640K and 1M.

- A *Coordinate* is an integer value that represents the horizontal or vertical location on the display screen. The *x* coordinate represents the location of a pixel on the horizontal plane (the column), whereas the *y* coordinate represents the location of a pixel on the vertical plane (the row). The PowerPack expects these coordinates to start at 0. For example, the pixel at the topmost, leftmost part of the screen is at location 0,0. In addition, there are two types of coordinates. *Screen coordinates* deal with the display screen as a whole; location 0,0 is always the topmost, leftmost pixel on the screen. *Viewport,* or *window coordinates,* however, relate to the location of the pixel within the window you are displaying. The topmost, leftmost pixel in the viewport is at viewport location 0,0 but can be located anywhere on the screen.

- The *CP* is the Cursor Position. This is an internal cursor variable maintained by the kernel. It specifies where on the screen the next text or graphics drawing operation will occur. It is not the mouse cursor. If the CP is not mentioned in a particular function, that function doesn't affect the CP.

INTRODUCTION TO GRAPHICS KERNEL FUNCTIONS

This chapter describes PowerPack's kernel routines. The kernel contains the basic functions required for graphics programming. Several functions in this chapter reference predefined structures and data types, which are found in the header file gxlib.h and shown in Appendix A. To access the functions covered in this chapter, add the gxlib.h file to each source file that calls these routines, and add the GX_CS.LIB file (for the small memory model) to your link list.

All samples in this chapter are complete, executable functions compiled in the small memory model. The one piece of source code missing from the samples is the PrintError function, which is shown in Appendix A. Functions that rely on other functions to operate have been noted in the text. Each sample displays the function being described in bold type.

GXCLEARDISPLAY

This function clears a given display page to the selected color. The entire display page is initialized quickly.

Syntax: `int far pascal gxClearDisplay(color, page)`

Parameter: `color`

Type: `int`

Description: Color with which to clear the page.

Parameter: `page`

Type: `int`

Description: Display page to clear.

Comments: Call `gxSetDisplay` and `gxSetMode` to set up the desired display mode before calling this function.

Return value: Success returns `gxSUCCESS`. Failure returns an error code (negative value).

See also: `gxClearVirtual, gxSetDisplay, gxSetMode`

Example:

```
/*------------------------------------------------------------

Filename: gxCD.C

Function: gxClearDisplay

Description: Clears the screen to red in 640x480x16
            color
```

```
Prerequisite Function(s): gxSetDisplay
                          gxSetMode

See PrintError() function described in Appendix A

-------------------------------------------------------*/

#include <stdio.h>
#include <stdlib.h>
#include <conio.h>

#include <gxlib.h>

void PrintError(char * funcName, int retCode);

void
main()
{
    int retValue;       /* Return value storage   */
    int dispMode;       /* 640x480x16 color       */
    int dispColor;      /* Display Color          */
    int dispPage;       /* Display Page           */

    /* Local initialization section */

    dispMode = gxVGA_12; /* Set up 640x480x16 colors */
    dispColor = gxRED;   /* Do a full red screen     */
    dispPage = 0;        /* Page 0                   */
    retValue = 0;        /* Start clean              */

    /* Mandatory kernel initialization */

    retValue = gxSetDisplay(dispMode);
    if(retValue < 0)
    {
        PrintError("gxSetDisplay", retValue);
        return;
    }

    /* Let's set up our desired video mode */

    retValue = gxSetMode(gxGRAPHICS);
    if(retValue < 0)
    {
        PrintError("gxSetMode", retValue);
        return;
    }
```

```
/* Okay, let's clear the screen to red */

retValue = gxClearDisplay(dispColor, dispPage);
if(retValue < 0)
{
    PrintError("gxClearDisplay", retValue);
    return;
}

/* wait for a user keypress, then clean up and exit*/

getch();

retValue = gxSetMode(gxTEXT);
if(retValue < 0)
{
    PrintError("gxSetMode", retValue);
    return;
}

return;
}
```

GXCLEARVIRTUAL

This function clears the virtual buffer to the desired color. The entire buffer is initialized.

Syntax: `int far pascal gxClearVirtual(vhPtr, color)`

Parameter: `vhPtr`

Type: `GXHEADER *`

Description: Pointer to `GXHEADER` structure.

Parameter: `color`

Type: `int`

Description: Color with which to clear the virtual buffer.

Comments: You must first create a virtual buffer by calling gxCreateVirtual. Refer to Appendix A for a listing of the GXHEADER structures and a listing of valid color constants.

Return value: Success returns gxSUCCESS. Failure returns an error code (negative value).

See also: gxCreateVirtual, gxGetImage, gxPutImage

Example:

```
/*---------------------------------------------------------


Filename: gxCV.C

Function: gxClearVirtual

Description: Clears the 640x480 virtual buffer to red

Prerequisite Function(s): gxSetDisplay
                          gxSetMode
                          gxCreateVirtual
                          gxDestroyVirtual

See PrintError() function described in Appendix A

---------------------------------------------------------*/

#include <stdio.h>
#include <stdlib.h>
#include <conio.h>

#include <gxlib.h>

void PrintError(char * funcName, int retCode);

/* Global variables here... */

GXHEADER vHeader;        /* Storage for header info  */

void
main()
{
```

```
int retValue;      /* Return value storage  */
int dispMode;      /* 640x480x16 color      */
int dispColor;     /* Display Color         */

/* Local initialization section */

dispMode = gxVGA_12;      /* Set up 640x480x16 colors*/
dispColor = gxLIGHTRED;   /* clear virtual to red    */
retValue = 0;             /* Start clean             */

/* Mandatory kernel initialization */

retValue = gxSetDisplay(dispMode);
if(retValue < 0)
{
    PrintError("gxSetDisplay", retValue);
    return;
}

/* Let's set up our desired video mode */

retValue = gxSetMode(gxGRAPHICS);
if(retValue < 0)
{
    PrintError("gxSetMode", retValue);
    return;
}

/*
   Create a virtual buffer in conventional memory
   that is 640 by 480 in pixels
*/

retValue = gxCreateVirtual(gxCMM, &vHeader,
                        dispMode, 640, 480);
if(retValue < 0)
{
    PrintError("gxCreateVirtual", retValue);
    return;
}

/*
   Once created, the virtual buffer is all
   zeros (black). Clear it to red
*/
```

```
retValue = gxClearVirtual(&vHeader, dispColor);
if(retValue < 0)
{
    PrintError("gxClearVirtual", retValue);
    return;
}

/* Show what we have done */

retValue = gxVirtualDisplay(&vHeader,
                            0,0, 0,0, 639,479, 0);

/* Wait for a user keypress, then clean up and exit*/

getch();

/* We should always deallocate the memory */

retValue = gxDestroyVirtual(&vHeader);
if(retValue < 0)
{
    PrintError("gxDestroyVirtual", retValue);
    return;
}

retValue = gxSetMode(gxTEXT);
if(retValue < 0)
{
    PrintError("gxSetMode", retValue);
    return;
}

return;
}
```

GXCREATEVIRTUAL

This function creates a virtual buffer for a given image type, based upon the image's height, width, and display type. This buffer is created in conventional memory.

Syntax: `int far pascal gxCreateVirtual(vType, vhPtr, dType, width, height)`

Parameter: `vType`

Type: `int`

Description: Virtual memory type.

Parameter: `vhPtr`

Type: `GXHEADER *`

Description: Location where virtual header is returned.

Parameter: `dType`

Type: `int`

Description: Display type for image.

Parameter: `width`

Type: `int`

Description: Width of image in pixels.

Parameter: `height`

Type: `int`

Description: Height of image in pixels.

Comments: Notice that the image type `dType` represents the pixel depth of the image. Be sure you use a display type that matches the pixel depth of the image you are displaying. Refer to `gxSetDisplay` for a listing of appropriate display types. Refer to Appendix A for a listing of the `GXHEADER` structures. Refer to `gxGetDisplayType` to find `width` and `height` for the display type `dType`. Use one of the following constants for the type of memory in which you want the virtual buffer to be allocated:

vType   Where the virtual buffer is created.

gxCMM   Create buffer in conventional memory.

Return value: Success returns gxSUCCESS. Failure returns an error code (negative value).

See also: gxClearVirtual, gxGetImage, gxPutImage, gxGetDisplayInfo

Example:

```
/*---------------------------------------------------------

Filename: gxCRV.C

Function: gxCreateVirtual

Description: Creates a 640x480x16 virtual buffer in
             conventional memory

Prerequisite Function(s): gxSetDisplay
                          gxSetMode

See PrintError() function described in Appendix A

---------------------------------------------------------*/

#include <stdio.h>
#include <stdlib.h>
#include <conio.h>

#include <gxlib.h>

void PrintError(char * funcName, int retCode);

/* Global variables here... */

GXHEADER vHeader;       /* Storage for header info  */

void
main()
{
    int retValue;       /* Return value storage     */
    int dispMode;       /* 640x480x16 color         */
```

```
/* Local initialization section */

dispMode = gxVGA_12; /* Set up 640x480x16 colors */
retValue = 0;         /* Start clean              */

/* Mandatory kernel initialization */

retValue = gxSetDisplay(dispMode);
if(retValue < 0)
{
    PrintError("gxSetDisplay", retValue);
    return;
}

/* Let's set up our desired video mode */

retValue = gxSetMode(gxGRAPHICS);
if(retValue < 0)
{
    PrintError("gxSetMode", retValue);
    return;
}

/*
   Create a virtual buffer in conventional memory
   that is 640 by 480 in pixels
*/

retValue = gxCreateVirtual(gxCMM, &vHeader,
                           dispMode, 640, 480);
if(retValue < 0)
{
    PrintError("gxCreateVirtual", retValue);
    return;
}

/* wait for a user keypress, then clean up and exit*/

printf("Virtual buffer created ... ");
printf("press any key to destroy it.\n");

getch();

/* We should always deallocate the memory */

retValue = gxDestroyVirtual(&vHeader);
```

```
    if(retValue < 0)
    {
        PrintError("gxDestroyVirtual", retValue);
        return;
    }

    retValue = gxSetMode(gxTEXT);
    if(retValue < 0)
    {
        PrintError("gxSetMode", retValue);
        return;
    }

    return;
}
```

GXDELAY

This function delays for a specified number of milliseconds (1/1,000). This can be used for accurate delays that remain constant across computer speeds.

Syntax: `int far pascal gxDelay(delay)`

Parameter: `delay`

Type: `int`

Description: The number of milliseconds to delay.

Comments: The delay is machine-independent, so that the same amount of time is used on a 286 and a 486 computer.

Return value: Success returns `gxSUCCESS`. Failure returns an error code (negative value).

See also: None.

Example:

```
/*------------------------------------------------------

Filename: gxDY.C

Function: gxDelay
```

```
Description: Delays for 3.275 seconds

Prerequisite Function(s): gxSetDisplay

See PrintError() function described in Appendix A

-----------------------------------------------------------*/
#include <stdio.h>
#include <stdlib.h>
#include <conio.h>

#include <gxlib.h>

void PrintError(char * funcName, int retCode);

void
main()
{
    int retValue;           /* Return value storage     */
    int dispMode;           /* 640x350x16 color         */

    /* Local initialization section */

    dispMode = gxEGA_10;  /* Set up 640x350x16 colors */
    retValue = 0;           /* Start clean              */

    /* Mandatory kernel initialization */

    retValue = gxSetDisplay(dispMode);
    if(retValue < 0)
    {
        PrintError("gxSetDisplay", retValue);
        return;
    }

    /* Delay for 3.275 seconds */

    printf("Beginning delay for 3.275 seconds ... ");

    retValue = gxDelay(3275);
    if(retValue < 0)
    {
        PrintError("gxDelay", retValue);
        return;
    }
```

```
/* Done */

printf("done.\n\n");

return;
}
```

GXDESTROYVIRTUAL

This function destroys a virtual buffer by freeing the memory allocated by a call to gxCreateVirtual. All virtual buffers created must be destroyed before exiting your program.

Syntax: `int far pascal gxDestroyVirtual(vhPtr)`

Parameter: `vhPtr`

Type: `GXHEADER *`

Description: Pointer to GXHEADER structure.

Comments: This function destroys any virtual buffer. Although any virtual memory allocated in conventional memory space is automatically deallocated by DOS when your application exits, you should deallocate conventional memory buffers. Refer to Appendix A for a listing of the GXHEADER structures.

Return value: Success returns gxSUCCESS. Failure returns an error code (negative value).

See also: gxCreateVirtual, gxGetImage, gxPutImage

Example:

```
/*- - - - - - - - - - - - - - - - - - - - - - - - - - - - - - - - - - - - - - - - -

Filename: gxDRV.C

Function: gxDestroyVirtual

Description: Destroys virtual buffer created by
            gxCreateVirtual

Prerequisite Function(s): gxSetDisplay
                          gxSetMode
                          gxCreateVirtual
```

See PrintError() function described in Appendix A

```
- - - - - - - - - - - - - - - - - - - - - - - - - - - - - - - - - - - - - - - - - - - - - - - - - - - - - -*/

#include <stdio.h>
#include <stdlib.h>
#include <conio.h>

#include <gxlib.h>

void PrintError(char * funcName, int retCode);

/* Global variables here... */

GXHEADER vHeader;          /* Storage for header info  */

void
main()
{
    int retValue;          /* Return value storage     */
    int dispMode;          /* 640x480x16 color         */

    /* Local initialization section */

    dispMode = gxVGA_12; /* Set up 640x480x16 colors */
    retValue = 0;          /* Start clean              */

    /* Mandatory kernel initialization */

    retValue = gxSetDisplay(dispMode);
    if(retValue < 0)
    {
        PrintError("gxSetDisplay", retValue);
        return;
    }

    /* Let's set up our desired video mode */

    retValue = gxSetMode(gxGRAPHICS);
    if(retValue < 0)
    {
        PrintError("gxSetMode", retValue);
        return;
    }

    /*
        Create a virtual buffer in conventional memory
```

```
                that is 640 by 480 in pixels
         */

         retValue = gxCreateVirtual(gxCMM, &vHeader,
                                    dispMode, 640, 480);
         if(retValue < 0)
         {
             PrintError("gxCreateVirtual", retValue);
             return;
         }

         /* wait for a user keypress, then clean up and exit */

         printf("Virtual buffer created ... ");
         printf("press any key to destroy it.\n");

         getch();

         /* We should always deallocate the memory */

         retValue = gxDestroyVirtual(&vHeader);
         if(retValue < 0)
         {
             PrintError("gxDestroyVirtual", retValue);
             return;
         }

         retValue = gxSetMode(gxTEXT);
         if(retValue < 0)
         {
             PrintError("gxSetMode", retValue);
             return;
         }

         return;
}
```

GXDISPLAYVIRTUAL

This function saves an image from the screen and places it in a
virtual buffer previously created by gxCreateVirtual. Although
this routine will save images of any size, it is designed to save larger
images.

Syntax: `int far pascal gxDisplayVirtual(x1, y1, x2, y2, page, vhPtr, vx, vy)`

Parameter: x1,y1

Type: `int`

Description: Upper-left corner of image to save.

Parameter: x2,y2

Type: `int`

Description: Lower-right corner of image to save.

Parameter: page

Type: `int`

Description: Page from which to save (usually zero).

Parameter: vhPtr

Type: GXHEADER *

Description: Location to store GXHEADER structure.

Parameter: vx,vy

Type: `int`

Description: Upper-left corner to place image at in virtual buffer.

Comments: You must call gxCreateVirtual to allocate a virtual buffer for storage of the image you are saving. Refer to gxVirtualDisplay to place a saved image on-screen. Refer to Appendix A for a listing of the GXHEADER structures.

Return value: Success returns gxSUCCESS. Failure returns an error code (negative value).

See also: gxCreateVirtual, gxVirtualDisplay, gxGetImage

Example:

```
/*- - - - - - - - - - - - - - - - - - - - - - - - - - - - - - - - - - - - - - - - - - - - - - - - - - - - - -

Filename: gxDV.C

Function: gxDisplayVirtual

Description: Creates virtual buffer, clears screen red,
             saves a 100x100 part of the screen, clears
             screen blue, places saved red square in
             upper-left corner of blue screen

Prerequisite Function(s): gxSetDisplay
                          gxSetMode
                          gxCreateVirtual
                          gxDestroyVirtual

See PrintError() function described in Appendix A

- - - - - - - - - - - - - - - - - - - - - - - - - - - - - - - - - - - - - - - - - - - - - - - - - - - - - - -*/

#include <stdio.h>
#include <stdlib.h>
#include <conio.h>

#include <gxlib.h>

void PrintError(char * funcName, int retCode);

/* Global variables here... */

GXHEADER vHeader;       /* Storage for header info  */

void
main()
{
    int retValue;       /* Return value storage     */
    int dispMode;       /* 640x480x16 color         */
    int dispColor;      /* Display Color            */
    int dispPage;       /* Display Page             */
```

```
/* Local initialization section */

dispMode = gxVGA_12;   /* Set up 640x480x16 colors */
dispColor = gxRED;     /* Do a full red screen     */
dispPage = 0;          /* Page 0                   */
retValue = 0;          /* Start clean              */

/* Mandatory kernel initialization */

retValue = gxSetDisplay(dispMode);
if(retValue < 0)
{
    PrintError("gxSetDisplay", retValue);
    return;
}

/* Let's set up our desired video mode */

retValue = gxSetMode(gxGRAPHICS);
if(retValue < 0)
{
    PrintError("gxSetMode", retValue);
    return;
}

/*
   Create a virtual buffer in conventional memory
   that is 100 by 100 in pixels
*/

retValue = gxCreateVirtual(gxCMM, &vHeader,
                           dispMode, 100, 100);
if(retValue < 0)
{
    PrintError("gxCreateVirtual", retValue);
    return;
}

/* Next, clear the screen to red */

retValue = gxClearDisplay(dispColor, dispPage);
if(retValue < 0)
{
    PrintError("gxClearDisplay", retValue);
    return;
}
```

```c
/*
   Save the first 100 pixels of the red screen
   in both horizontal and vertical direction
*/

retValue = gxDisplayVirtual(0,0, 99,99, 0, &vHeader,
                            0,0);
if(retValue < 0)
{
    PrintError("gxDisplayVirtual", retValue);
    return;
}

/* wait for first user keypress */

getch();

/* Next, clear the screen to blue */

retValue = gxClearDisplay(gxBLUE, dispPage);
if(retValue < 0)
{
    PrintError("gxClearDisplay", retValue);
    return;
}

/* wait for second user keypress */

getch();

/*
   Put the red saved block over the blue screen
   in upper-left corner of the screen
*/

retValue = gxVirtualDisplay(&vHeader,
                            0,0, 0,0, 99,99, 0);
if(retValue < 0)
{
    PrintError("gxVirtualDisplay", retValue);
    return;
}

/* wait for last user keypress, then clean up and
   exit */
```

```
getch();

/* We should always deallocate the memory */

retValue = gxDestroyVirtual(&vHeader);
if(retValue < 0)
{
    PrintError("gxDestroyVirtual", retValue);
    return;
}

retValue = gxSetMode(gxTEXT);
if(retValue < 0)
{
    PrintError("gxSetMode", retValue);
    return;
}

return;
}
```

GXGETDISPLAY

This function returns the current kernel display type previously defined by the last call to gxSetDisplay.

Syntax: int far pascal gxGetDisplay(void)

Parameters: None.

Comments: The return value is one of the constants shown in the first column of the following list.

Return Value	Mode Type	Mode Number	Resolution
gxEGA_D	EGA	0D hex	320x200x16
gxEGA_E	EGA	0E hex	640x200x16
gxEGA_F	EGA	0F hex	640x350x2
gxEGA_10	EGA	10 hex	640x350x16
gxVGA_11	VGA	11 hex	640x480x2
gxVGA_12	VGA	12 hex	640x480x16

Return value: One of the constants shown in the preceding list.

See also: gxSetDisplay, gxSetMode, gxGetDisplayInfo

Example:

```
/*-----------------------------------------------------------

Filename: gxGD.C

Function: gxGetDisplay

Description: Gets the display type for 640x480x16 color

Prerequisite Function(s): gxSetDisplay

See PrintError() function described in Appendix A

-----------------------------------------------------------*/

#include <stdio.h>
#include <stdlib.h>
#include <conio.h>

#include <gxlib.h>

void PrintError(char * funcName, int retCode);

void
main()
{
    int retValue;        /* Return value storage    */
    int dispMode;        /* 640x480x16 color        */

    /* Local initialization section */

    dispMode = gxVGA_12; /* Set up 640x480x16 colors */
    retValue = 0;          /* Start clean              */

    /* Mandatory kernel initialization */

    retValue = gxSetDisplay(dispMode);
    if(retValue < 0)
    {
        PrintError("gxSetDisplay", retValue);
        return;
```

```
    }

    /* Get the current display type */

    retValue = gxGetDisplay();
    if(retValue < 0)
    {
        PrintError("gxGetDisplay", retValue);
        return;
    }

    /* Print the display type */

    printf("\ngxGetDisplay returned %d.\n", retValue);

    return;
}
```

GXGETDISPLAYINFO

This function returns information about the desired display type.

Syntax: `int far pascal gxGetDisplayInfo(dType, di)`

Parameter: `dType`

Type: `int`

Description: Display mode type.

Parameter: `di`

Type: `GXDINFO *`

Description: Location to store `GXDINFO` structure.

Comments: The information about the `dType` display type is returned to a structure pointed to by `di`. This function is especially useful for determining needed information about the display mode for routines such as `gxCreateVirtual`. Refer to Appendix A for a listing of the `GXDINFO` structures. Refer to `gxSetDisplay` for a listing of display types for `dType`.

Return value: Success returns gxSUCCESS. Failure returns an error code (negative value).

See also: gxSetDisplay, gxSetMode, gxCreateVirtual

Example:

```
/*-------------------------------------------------------

Filename: gxGDI.C

Function: gxGetDisplayInfo

Description: Gets detailed information about mode
            640x480x16

Prerequisite Function(s): gxSetDisplay

See PrintError() function described in Appendix A

-------------------------------------------------------*/

#include <stdio.h>
#include <stdlib.h>
#include <conio.h>

#include <gxlib.h>

void PrintError(char * funcName, int retCode);

/* Global variables here... */

GXDINFO dispInfo;

void
main()
{
    int retValue;        /* Return value storage     */
    int dispMode;        /* 640x480x16 color         */

    /* Local initialization section */

    dispMode = gxVGA_12; /* Set up 640x480x16 colors */
    retValue = 0;        /* Start clean              */

    /* Mandatory kernel initialization */
```

```
retValue = gxSetDisplay(dispMode);
if(retValue < 0)
{
    PrintError("gxSetDisplay", retValue);
    return;
}

/* Get the current display type */

retValue = gxGetDisplayInfo(dispMode, &dispInfo);
if(retValue < 0)
{
    PrintError("gxGetDisplayInfo", retValue);
    return;
}

/*
    Print the display type information,
    and exit
*/

printf("\ngxGetDisplayInfo returned:\n\n");

printf("Display mode type     = %d\n",
                        dispInfo.dtype);
printf("String Description    = %s\n",
                        dispInfo.descrip);
printf("BIOS Video Mode Num   = %x hex\n",
                        dispInfo.mode);
printf("Pixel Depth           = %d\n",
                        dispInfo.bitpx);
printf("Horizontal Res        = %d\n",
                        dispInfo.hres);
printf("Vertical Res          = %d\n",
                        dispInfo.vres);
printf("# of Bytes per Row    = %d\n",
                        dispInfo.bplin);
printf("# of Display Planes   = %d\n",
                        dispInfo.planes);
printf("# of Display Pages    = %d\n",
                        dispInfo.pages);
printf("Beginning Display Seg = %X hex\n",
                        dispInfo.begseg);
printf("Display Page Size     = %d\n",
                        dispInfo.pagesize);
printf("Palette Format Type   = %d\n\n",
                        dispInfo.paltype);
```

```
        return;
}
```

GXGETDISPLAYPALETTE

This function returns the current display color palette to a specified buffer. The number of bytes required to store the palette is dependent on the current display type.

Syntax: `int far pascal gxGetDisplayPalette(pal)`

Parameter: `pal`

Type: `char *`

Description: Buffer to store the current display palette.

Comments: The number of bytes returned is a function of the current display type. The following list shows the amount of memory you must allocate to store the palette for each display type.

Display Type	Mode Type	Memory need
gxEGA_D	EGA	17 bytes
gxEGA_E	EGA	17 bytes
gxEGA_F	EGA	17 bytes
gxEGA_10	EGA	17 bytes
gxVGA_11	VGA	48 bytes
gxVGA_12	VGA	48 bytes

Return value: Success returns `gxSUCCESS`. Failure returns an error code (negative value).

See also: `gxSetDisplayPalette`, `gxGetDisplay`, `gxGetDisplayInfo`

Example:

```
/*-----------------------------------------------------

Filename: gxGDP.C

Function: gxGetDisplayPalette
```

```
Description: Gets color palette values for mode
             640x480x16

Prerequisite Function(s): gxSetDisplay
                          gxSetMode       .

See PrintError() function described in Appendix A

---------------------------------------------------------*/

#include <stdio.h>
#include <stdlib.h>
#include <conio.h>

#include <gxlib.h>

void PrintError(char * funcName, int retCode);

/* Global variables here... */

/* Buffer to hold color palette values */
char cPalette[48];     /* Need 48 bytes for gxVGA_12 */

void
main()
{
    int retValue;      /* Return value storage    */
    int dispMode;      /* 640x480x16 color        */
    int idx;           /* Index counter           */

    /* Local initialization section */

    dispMode = gxVGA_12; /* Set up 640x480x16 colors */
    retValue = 0;        /* Start clean              */

    /* Mandatory kernel initialization */

    retValue = gxSetDisplay(dispMode);
    if(retValue < 0)
    {
        PrintError("gxSetDisplay", retValue);
        return;
    }

    /* Let's set up our desired video mode */
```

```
retValue = gxSetMode(gxGRAPHICS);
if(retValue < 0)
{
    PrintError("gxSetMode", retValue);
    return;
}

/* Get the current display palette */

retValue = gxGetDisplayPalette(cPalette);
if(retValue < 0)
{
    PrintError("gxGetDisplayPalette", retValue);
    return;
}

/*
    Print each of the 16 colors in RED, GREEN, BLUE
    order.
*/

for(idx= 0; idx < 48; idx += 3)
{

    printf("Palette %2d: ",idx/3);
    printf("Red: %2d, Green: %2d, Blue: %2d\n",
      cPalette[idx], cPalette[idx+1],
      cPalette[idx+2]);

}

printf("\nHit any key to exit... ");

getch();
putchar('\n');

/* Clean up and exit */

retValue = gxSetMode(gxTEXT);
if(retValue < 0)
{
    PrintError("gxSetMode", retValue);
    return;
}


return;
}
```

GXGETIMAGE

This function saves an image from the screen and places it in a virtual buffer previously created by gxCreateVirtual. This routine is designed to save images of less than 64K. For larger images, refer to gxDisplayVirtual.

Syntax: `int far pascal gxGetImage(vhPtr, x1, y1, x2, y2, page)`

Parameter: vhPtr

Type: GXHEADER *

Description: Location to store GXHEADER structure.

Parameter: x1,y1

Type: int

Description: Upper-left corner of the image to save.

Parameter: x2,y2

Type: int

Description: Lower-right corner of the image to save.

Parameter: page

Type: int

Description: Page from which to save (usually zero).

Comments: You must call gxCreateVirtual to allocate a virtual buffer for storage of the image you are saving. Refer to gxPutImage to place a saved image on-screen. Refer to Appendix A for a listing of the GXHEADER structures.

Return value: Success returns gxSUCCESS. Failure returns an error code (negative value).

See also: gxCreateVirtual, gxDisplayVirtual, gxPutImage

Example:

```
/*----------------------------------------------------------

Filename: gxGI.C

Function: gxGetImage

Description: Creates virtual buffer, clears screen red,
             saves a 100x100 part of the screen, clears
             screen blue, places saved red square in
             upper-left corner of blue screen

Prerequisite Function(s): gxSetDisplay
                          gxSetMode
                          gxCreateVirtual
                          gxDestroyVirtual

See PrintError() function described in Appendix A

----------------------------------------------------------*/

#include <stdio.h>
#include <stdlib.h>
#include <conio.h>

#include <gxlib.h>

void PrintError(char * funcName, int retCode);

/* Global variables here... */

GXHEADER vHeader;       /* Storage for header info  */

void
main()
{
    int retValue;       /* Return value storage     */
    int dispMode;       /* 640x480x16 color         */
    int dispColor;      /* Display Color            */
    int dispPage;       /* Display Page             */
```

```
/* Local initialization section */

dispMode = gxVGA_12; /* Set up 640x480x16 colors */
dispColor = gxRED;   /* Do a full red screen     */
dispPage = 0;        /* Page 0                   */
retValue = 0;        /* Start clean              */

/* Mandatory kernel initialization */

retValue = gxSetDisplay(dispMode);
if(retValue < 0)
{
    PrintError("gxSetDisplay", retValue);
    return;
}

/* Let's set up our desired video mode */

retValue = gxSetMode(gxGRAPHICS);
if(retValue < 0)
{
    PrintError("gxSetMode", retValue);
    return;
}

/*
   Create a virtual buffer in conventional memory
   that is 100 by 100 in pixels
*/

retValue = gxCreateVirtual(gxCMM, &vHeader,
                           dispMode, 100, 100);
if(retValue < 0)
{
    PrintError("gxCreateVirtual", retValue);
    return;
}

/* Next, clear the screen to red */

retValue = gxClearDisplay(dispColor, dispPage);
if(retValue < 0)
{
    PrintError("gxClearDisplay", retValue);
    return;
}
```

```
/*
    Save the first 100 pixels of the red screen
    in both horizontal and vertical directions
*/

retValue = gxGetImage(&vHeader, 0,0, 100,100, 0);
if(retValue < 0)
{
    PrintError("gxGetImage", retValue);
    return;
}

/* wait for first user keypress */

getch();

/* Next, clear the screen to blue */

retValue = gxClearDisplay(gxBLUE, dispPage);
if(retValue < 0)
{
    PrintError("gxClearDisplay", retValue);
    return;
}

/* wait for second user keypress */

getch();

/*
    Put the red saved block over the blue screen
    in upper-left corner of the screen
*/

retValue = gxPutImage(&vHeader, gxSET, 0,0, 0);
if(retValue < 0)
{
    PrintError("gxPutImage", retValue);
    return;
}

    /* wait for last user keypress, then clean up and
exit */
```

```
    getch();

    /* We should always deallocate the memory */

    retValue = gxDestroyVirtual(&vHeader);
    if(retValue < 0)
    {
        PrintError("gxDestroyVirtual", retValue);
        return;
    }

    retValue = gxSetMode(gxTEXT);
    if(retValue < 0)
    {
        PrintError("gxSetMode", retValue);
        return;
    }

    return;
}
```

GXGETPAGE

This function returns the current display page (the first page is page zero).

Syntax: `int far pascal gxGetPage(void)`

Parameters: None.

Comments: The number of available display pages differs with each display type. Refer to `gxSetPage` for a listing of display page availability for each display type.

Return value: Success returns the current display page. Failure returns an error code (negative value).

See also: `gxSetPage`

Example:

```
/*-------------------------------------------------------

Filename: gxGP.C

Function: gxGetPage
```

```
Description: Gets the current active page for 640x480x16

Prerequisite Function(s): gxSetDisplay

See PrintError() function described in Appendix A

-------------------------------------------------------*/

#include <stdio.h>
#include <stdlib.h>
#include <conio.h>

#include <gxlib.h>

void PrintError(char * funcName, int retCode);

void
main()
{
    int retValue;        /* Return value storage   */
    int dispMode;        /* 640x480x16 color       */

    /* Local initialization section */

    dispMode = gxVGA_12; /* Set up 640x480x16 colors */
    retValue = 0;        /* Start clean              */

    /* Mandatory kernel initialization */

    retValue = gxSetDisplay(dispMode);
    if(retValue < 0)
    {
        PrintError("gxSetDisplay", retValue);
        return;
    }

    /* Let's set up our desired video mode */

    retValue = gxSetMode(gxGRAPHICS);
    if(retValue < 0)
    {
        PrintError("gxSetMode", retValue);
        return;
    }

    /* Get the current display page */
```

```
retValue = gxGetPage();
if(retValue < 0)
{
    PrintError("gxGetPage", retValue);
    return;
}

/*
    Print the page count, wait for a keypress,
    then exit
*/

printf("\ngxGetPage returned page %d", retValue);
printf("\nHit any key to exit... ");

getch();
putchar('\n');

/* Let's reset to text mode */

retValue = gxSetMode(gxTEXT);
if(retValue < 0)
{
    PrintError("gxSetMode", retValue);
    return;
}

return;
}
```

GXGETPALETTECOLOR

This function returns the palette color that resides at a specified index location.

Syntax: `int far pascal gxGetPaletteColor(index)`

Parameter: `index`

Type: `int`

Description: The palette index value (0-15).

Comments: This function returns the palette values for EGA modes only. Because only 16 colors are available in EGA mode, the index argument range is limited to 0 to 15. Refer to gxGetPaletteRGB to retrieve colors for VGA modes.

Return value: The return value is the desired palette color.

See also: gxGetPaletteRGB, gxDisplayPalette, gxGetDisplayInfo

Example:

```
/*------------------------------------------------------------

Filename: gxGPC.C

Function: gxGetPaletteColor

Description: Gets color for index 12 of EGA 640x350x16

Prerequisite Function(s): gxSetDisplay
                          gxGetDisplayPalette

See PrintError() function described in Appendix A

------------------------------------------------------------*/

#include <stdio.h>
#include <stdlib.h>
#include <conio.h>

#include <gxlib.h>

void PrintError(char * funcName, int retCode);

void
main()
{
    int retValue;        /* Return value storage    */
    int dispMode;        /* 640x350x16 color        */
    int idx;             /* Index counter           */

    /* Local initialization section */

    dispMode = gxEGA_10; /* Set up 640x350x16 colors */
    idx      = 12;       /* Color palette 12         */
    retValue = 0;        /* Start clean              */
```

```
    /* Mandatory kernel initialization */

    retValue = gxSetDisplay(dispMode);
    if(retValue < 0)
    {
        PrintError("gxSetDisplay", retValue);
        return;
    }

    /* Let's set up our desired video mode */

    retValue = gxSetMode(gxGRAPHICS);
    if(retValue < 0)
    {
        PrintError("gxSetMode", retValue);
        return;
    }

    /* Get the current palette color */

    retValue = gxGetPaletteColor(idx);
    if(retValue < 0)
    {
        PrintError("gxGetPaletteColor", retValue);
        return;
    }

    printf("gxGetPaletteColor 12 = %d\n", retValue);
    printf("\nHit any key to exit... ");

    getch();
    putchar('\n');

    /* Clean up and exit */

    retValue = gxSetMode(gxTEXT);
    if(retValue < 0)
    {
        PrintError("gxSetMode", retValue);
        return;
    }


    return;
}
```

GxGetPaletteRGB

This function returns red, green, and blue component values for the desired index.

Syntax: `int far pascal gxGetPaletteRGB(index, red, green, blue)`

Parameter: `index`

Type: `int`

Description: The palette index value (0-255).

Parameter: `red`

Type: `int *`

Description: Storage location for the red color component.

Parameter: `green`

Type: `int *`

Description: Storage location for the green color component.

Parameter: `blue`

Type: `int *`

Description: Storage location for the blue color component.

Comments: This function returns the palette values for VGA modes only. Because there are 16 colors in the palette, the `index` argument range is limited to 0 to 15. At each palette index are three color components—red, green, and `blue`—that make up the actual color displayed. Palette index zero is usually set to black (`red=0`, `green=0`, `blue=0`). Each color component has a range of 0 to 63. Refer to `gxGetPaletteColor` to retrieve colors for EGA modes.

Return value: Success returns gxSUCCESS. Failure returns an error code (negative value).

See also: gxGetPaletteColor, gxDisplayPalette, gxGetDisplayInfo

Example:

```
/*------------------------------------------------- ----------

Filename: gxGPRGB.C

Function: gxGetPaletteRGB

Description: Gets red, green, and blue component color
            values for index 12 of VGA 640x480x16

Prerequisite Function(s): gxSetDisplay
                          gxGetDisplayPalette
                          gxGetDisplayColor

See PrintError() function described in Appendix A

----------------------------------------------------------*/

#include <stdio.h>
#include <stdlib.h>
#include <conio.h>

#include <gxlib.h>

void PrintError(char * funcName, int retCode);

void
main()
{
    int retValue;          /* Return value storage    */
    int dispMode;          /* 640x480x16 color        */
    int idx;               /* Index counter           */
    int red, green, blue;  /* Component color values  */

    /* Local initialization section */

    dispMode = gxVGA_12;   /* Set up 640x480x16 color */
    idx      = 12;         /* Color palette 12        */
    retValue = 0;          /* Start clean             */
```

```
/* Mandatory kernel initialization */

retValue = gxSetDisplay(dispMode);
if(retValue < 0)
{
    PrintError("gxSetDisplay", retValue);
    return;
}

/* Let's set up our desired video mode */

retValue = gxSetMode(gxGRAPHICS);
if(retValue < 0)
{
    PrintError("gxSetMode", retValue);
    return;
}

/* Get the current RGB color */

retValue = gxGetPaletteRGB(idx, &red, &green,
                            &blue);
if(retValue < 0)
{
    PrintError("gxGetPaletteRGB", retValue);
    return;
}

printf("gxGetPaletteRGB %02d = %02d (red),\n", idx,
        red);
printf("                        %02d (green),\n",
        green);
printf("                        %02d (blue)\n", blue);
printf("\nHit any key to exit... ");

getch();
putchar('\n');

/* Clean up and exit */

retValue = gxSetMode(gxTEXT);
if(retValue < 0)
{
    PrintError("gxSetMode", retValue);
    return;
}
```

```
    return;
}
```

GxGetRandom

This function returns a random number whose range is from zero to a specified maximum minus one.

Syntax: `int far pascal gxGetRandom(range)`

Parameter: `range`

Type: `int`

Description: The range of possible random numbers.

Comments: This function doesn't return fractional numbers—it returns only integers. The random number is in the range of zero to `range` minus one. The `gxGetRandom` function is used to produce random numbers for such applications as a game or random colors.

Return value: Returns a random number from zero to `range` minus one.

See also: `gxSetDisplay, gxSetMode`

Example:

```
/*------------------------------------------------------------

Filename: gxGR.C

Function: gxGetRandom

Description: Gets a pseudo-random number. However, each
            time you run this program, you will get the
            same random numbers. Call gxSetRandom,
            using the time of day in seconds, each time
            you start the program, and it will be more
            random.

Prerequisite Function(s): gxSetDisplay

See PrintError() function described in Appendix A
```

```
- - - - - - - - - - - - - - - - - - - - - - - - - - - - - - - - - - - - - - - - - - - - - - - - - -*/

#include <stdio.h>
#include <stdlib.h>
#include <conio.h>

#include <gxlib.h>

void PrintError(char * funcName, int retCode);

void
main()
{
    int retValue;        /* Return value storage    */
    int dispMode;        /* 640x480x16 color        */
    int range;           /* random maximum value    */
    int cnt;             /* random numbers loop      */

    /* Local initialization section */

    dispMode = gxVGA_12; /* Set up 640x480x16 colors */
    range    = 256;      /* random must be < 256    */
    cnt      = 5;        /* do 5 random numbers     */
    retValue = 0;        /* start clean             */


    /* Mandatory kernel initialization */

    retValue = gxSetDisplay(dispMode);
    if(retValue < 0)
    {
        PrintError("gxSetDisplay", retValue);
        return;
    }

    for(; cnt > 0; cnt--)
    {
        retValue = gxGetRandom(range);
        if(retValue < 0)
        {
            PrintError("gxGetRandom", retValue);
            return;
        }
        printf("Random number is %d\n", retValue);
    }
```

```
    return;
}
```

GXPUTIMAGE

This function places on the display screen an image residing in a virtual buffer. It is designed to place images of less than 64K, and it is capable of performing logical operations.

Syntax: `int far pascal gxPutImage(vhPtr, op, x, y, page)`

Parameter: `vhPtr`

Type: `GXHEADER *`

Description: Pointer to `GXHEADER` structure.

Parameter: `op`

Type: `int`

Description: Bitwise operations on the image.

Parameter: `x,y`

Type: `int`

Description: Upper-left corner of the screen on which to place an image.

Parameter: `page`

Type: `int`

Description: Page on which to place an image.

Comments: You must first place an image into `vhPtr` by calling `gxGetImage` or by some other means. Refer to Appendix A for a listing of the `GXHEADER` structures. The `op` argument specifies bitwise operations that can be performed on the image as it is placed on the display. The following list contains the valid operations.

Bitwise Operation Desired	Argument Constant to use
Set/Replace all display pixels with image	gxSET
Bitwise AND the image with the display	gxAND
Bitwise OR the image with the display	gxOR
Bitwise XOR the image with the display	gxXOR

Return value: Success returns gxSUCCESS. Failure returns an error code (negative value).

See also: gxCreateVirtual, gxGetImage

Example:

```
/*-------------------------------------------------------

Filename: gxPI.C

Function: gxPutImage

Description: Creates virtual buffer, clears screen red,
             saves a 100x100 part of the screen, clears
             screen blue, and places the saved red
             squares in the four corners of the blue
             screen

Prerequisite Function(s): gxSetDisplay
                          gxSetMode
                          gxCreateVirtual
                          gxDestroyVirtual
                          gxGetImage

See PrintError() function described in Appendix A

-------------------------------------------------------*/

#include <stdio.h>
#include <stdlib.h>
#include <conio.h>
```

```
#include <gxlib.h>

void PrintError(char * funcName, int retCode);

/* Global variables here... */

GXHEADER vHeader;           /* Storage for header info  */

void
main()
{
    int retValue;           /* Return value storage     */
    int dispMode;           /* 640x480x16 color         */
    int dispColor;          /* Display Color            */

    int dispPage;           /* Display Page             */

    /* Local initialization section */

    dispMode = gxVGA_12; /* Set up 640x480x16 colors */
    dispColor = gxRED;   /* Do a full red screen     */
    dispPage = 0;        /* Page 0                   */
    retValue = 0;        /* Start clean              */

    /* Mandatory kernel initialization */

    retValue = gxSetDisplay(dispMode);
    if(retValue < 0)
    {
        PrintError("gxSetDisplay", retValue);
        return;
    }

    /* Let's set up our desired video mode */

    retValue = gxSetMode(gxGRAPHICS);
    if(retValue < 0)
    {
        PrintError("gxSetMode", retValue);
        return;
    }

    /*
        Create a virtual buffer in conventional memory
        that is 100 by 100 in pixels
    */
```

```
retValue = gxCreateVirtual(gxCMM, &vHeader,
                           dispMode, 100, 100);
if(retValue < 0)
{
    PrintError("gxCreateVirtual", retValue);
    return;
}

/* Next, clear the screen to red */

retValue = gxClearDisplay(dispColor, dispPage);
if(retValue < 0)
{
    PrintError("gxClearDisplay", retValue);
    return;
}

/*
   Save the first 100 pixels of the red screen
   in both horizontal and vertical directions
*/

retValue = gxGetImage(&vHeader, 0,0, 99,99, 0);
if(retValue < 0)
{
    PrintError("gxGetImage", retValue);
    return;
}

/* wait for first user keypress */

getch();

/* Next, clear the screen to blue */

retValue = gxClearDisplay(gxBLUE, dispPage);
if(retValue < 0)
{
    PrintError("gxClearDisplay", retValue);
    return;
}

/* wait for second user keypress */

getch();
```

```c
/*
    Put the red saved block over the blue screen
    in upper-left corner of the screen
*/

retValue = gxPutImage(&vHeader, gxSET, 0,0, 0);
if(retValue < 0)
{
    PrintError("gxPutImage", retValue);
    return;
}

/* wait for third user keypress */

getch();

/*
    Put the red saved block over the blue screen
    in lower-left corner of the screen
*/

retValue = gxPutImage(&vHeader, gxSET, 0,380, 0);
if(retValue < 0)
{
    PrintError("gxPutImage", retValue);
    return;
}

/* wait for fourth user keypress */

getch();

/*
    Put the red saved block over the blue screen
    in upper-right corner of the screen
*/

retValue = gxPutImage(&vHeader, gxSET, 540,0, 0);
if(retValue < 0)
{
    PrintError("gxPutImage", retValue);
    return;
}

/* wait for fifth user keypress */
```

```
getch();

/*
   Put the red saved block over the blue screen
   in lower-right corner of the screen
*/

retValue = gxPutImage(&vHeader, gxSET, 540,380, 0);
if(retValue < 0)
{
    PrintError("gxPutImage", retValue);
    return;
}

/* wait for last user keypress, then clean up and
   exit */

getch();

/* Always deallocate the memory */

retValue = gxDestroyVirtual(&vHeader);
if(retValue < 0)
{
    PrintError("gxDestroyVirtual", retValue);
    return;
}

retValue = gxSetMode(gxTEXT);
if(retValue < 0)
{
    PrintError("gxSetMode", retValue);
    return;
}

    return;
}
```

GXSETBUFFER

This function defines a buffer to be used by the kernel in addition
to the kernel's internal buffer. This is desirable for operations that
require larger buffers (functions such as grFloodFill), or to speed
up file access (for functions like pcxFileImage).

Syntax: `int far pascal gxSetBuffer(buf, bufmax)`

Parameter: `buf`

Type: `char *`

Description: Buffer to be set aside for kernel usage.

Parameter: `bufmax`

Type: `int`

Description: Maximum number of bytes used in the buffer.

Comments: This function does *not* allocate memory. It simply tells the kernel it can use this memory (allocated by you). Call this function again with `bufmax` set to zero to tell the kernel to stop using your buffer. You are responsible for freeing up the buffer memory. Also, do *not* use a locally allocated buffer in your function or on the stack. Make sure the memory is allocated globally before calling `gxSetBuffer`. Local allocation will result in a memory overwrite, which will crash your computer.

Return value: Success returns `gxSUCCESS`. Failure returns an error code (negative value).

See also: `gxCreateVirtual, gxDestroyVirtual`

Example:

```
/*- - - - - - - - - - - - - - - - - - - - - - - - - - - - - - - - - - - - - - - - - - - - - - -

Filename: gxSB.C

Function: gxSetBuffer

Description: Defines a 20,000 byte buffer to be used
            internally by the kernel. A more useful
            example is shown in the function
            grFloodFill in the next chapter

Prerequisite Function(s): gxSetDisplay

See PrintError() function described in Appendix A

- - - - - - - - - - - - - - - - - - - - - - - - - - - - - - - - - - - - - - - - - - - - - - -*/
```

```
#include <stdio.h>
#include <stdlib.h>
#include <conio.h>

#include <gxlib.h>

void PrintError(char * funcName, int retCode);

/* Global variables here... */

#define SBUFSIZE    20000 /* Size of additional buffer*/

char kernelBuf[SBUFSIZE]; /* Storage for header info  */
                          /* MUST be in global memory */

void
main()
{
    int retValue;          /* Return value storage   */
    int dispMode;          /* 640x480x16 color       */

    /* Local initialization section */

    dispMode = gxVGA_12;   /* Set up 640x480x16 colors*/
    retValue = 0;          /* Start clean             */

    /* Mandatory kernel initialization */

    retValue = gxSetDisplay(dispMode);
    if(retValue < 0)
    {
        PrintError("gxSetDisplay", retValue);
        return;
    }

    /*
        Use this function to inform the kernel to
        use this buffer in addition to the internal
        buffer for large operations.
    */

    retValue = gxSetBuffer(kernelBuf, SBUFSIZE);
    if(retValue < 0)
    {
```

```
        PrintError("gxSetBuffer", retValue);
        return;
    }

    /* wait for user keypress, then exit */

    printf("Internal buffer set. Hit any key to exit...
            ");

    getch();
    putchar('\n');


    return;
}
```

GXSETDISPLAY

This function initializes the kernel's internal data structures. It doesn't alter the current display mode but prepares the kernel for future graphics operations.

Syntax: `int far pascal gxSetDisplay(dType)`

Parameter: `dType`

Type: `int`

Description: Display type to use for kernel initialization.

Comments: Use one of the following constants for the `dType` argument:

dType	Mode Type	Mode Number	Resolution
gxEGA_D	EGA	0D hex	320x200x16
gxEGA_E	EGA	0E hex	640x200x16
gxEGA_F	EGA	0F hex	640x350x2
gxEGA_10	EGA	10 hex	640x350x16
gxVGA_11	VGA	11 hex	640x480x2
gxVGA_12	VGA	12 hex	640x480x16

Return value: Success returns `gxSUCCESS`. Failure returns an error code (negative value).

See also: gxSetMode, gxGetDisplay

Example:

```
/*-------------------------------------------------------

Filename: gxSD.C

Function: gxSetDisplay

Description: Sets up kernel's internal data structures
            for future function calls for entire
            package

Prerequisite Function(s): None, this is it

See PrintError() function described in Appendix A

-----------------------------------------------------*/

#include <stdio.h>
#include <stdlib.h>
#include <conio.h>

#include <gxlib.h>

void PrintError(char * funcName, int retCode);

void
main()
{
    int retValue;       /* Return value storage   */
    int dispMode;       /* 640x480x16 color       */

    /* Local initialization section */

    dispMode = gxVGA_12; /* Set up 640x480x16 colors */
    retValue = 0;        /* Start clean              */

    /* Mandatory kernel initialization */

    retValue = gxSetDisplay(dispMode);
    if(retValue < 0)
    {
        PrintError("gxSetDisplay", retValue);
        return;
    }
```

```
    printf("Display type set successfully.\n");

    return;
}
```

GXSETDISPLAYPALETTE

This function sets the display palette according to the current display type set by gxSetDisplay. The argument is expected to be in the format returned from a call to gxGetDisplayPalette.

Syntax: `int far pascal gxSetDisplayPalette(pal)`

Parameter: `pal`

Type: `char *`

Description: Pointer to display palette.

Comments: Setting the palette colors should be done after setting the display mode (using `gxSetMode`, for example) because a set mode forces the palette to default colors.

Return value: Success returns `gxSUCCESS`. Failure returns an error code (negative value).

See also: `gxGetDisplayPalette, gxGetDisplay, gxGetDisplayInfo`

Example:

```
/*---------------------------------------------------------

Filename: gxSDP.C

Function: gxSetDisplayPalette

Description: Fills a palette buffer with a green ramp,
            and prints the ramp on the screen

Prerequisite Function(s): gxSetDisplay
                          gxSetMode
                          gxGetDisplayPalette

See PrintError() function described in Appendix A

-----------------------------------------------------*/
```

```c
#include <stdio.h>
#include <stdlib.h>
#include <conio.h>

#include <gxlib.h>

void PrintError(char * funcName, int retCode);

/* Global variables here... */

/* Buffer to hold color palette values */
char cPalette[48];       /* Need 48 bytes for gxVGA_12 */

void
main()
{
    int retValue;       /* Return value storage    */
    int dispMode;       /* 640x480x16 color        */
    int idx;            /* Index counter           */

    /* Local initialization section */

    dispMode = gxVGA_12; /* Set up 640x480x16 colors */
    retValue = 0;        /* Start clean              */


    /* Mandatory kernel initialization */

    retValue = gxSetDisplay(dispMode);
    if(retValue < 0)
    {
        PrintError("gxSetDisplay", retValue);
        return;
    }

    /* Let's set up our desired video mode */

    retValue = gxSetMode(gxGRAPHICS);
    if(retValue < 0)
    {
        PrintError("gxSetMode", retValue);
        return;
    }
```

```
/*
   Setup the local palette buffer so
   that it is a green color ramp
*/

for(idx = 0; idx < 48; idx += 3)
{
    cPalette[idx] = (char) 0;
    cPalette[idx+1] = (char) ((idx / 3) * 4);
    cPalette[idx+2] = (char) 0;
}

/*
   Copy this local palette into the system
   palette.
*/

retValue = gxSetDisplayPalette(cPalette);
if(retValue < 0)
{
    PrintError("gxSetDisplayPalette", retValue);
    return;
}

for(idx=0; idx < 16; idx++)
{
    retValue = gxClearDisplay(idx, 0);
    if(retValue < 0)
    {
        PrintError("gxClearDisplay", retValue);
        return;
    }
}

/* Wait for a key */
getch();

/* Clean up and exit */

retValue = gxSetMode(gxTEXT);
if(retValue < 0)
{
    PrintError("gxSetMode", retValue);
    return;
}
```

```
    return;
}
```

GXSETMODE

This function alters the current display mode, changing it to the display type specified by the argument.

Syntax: `int far pascal gxSetMode(gxMode)`

Parameter: `gxMode`

Type: `int`

Description: `gxGRAPHICS` or `gxTEXT`

Comments: Use the constant `gxGRAPHICS` to force the display mode to the mode previously defined by calling `gxSetDisplay` or use `gxTEXT` to return to normal text display mode.

Return value: Success returns `gxSUCCESS`. Failure returns an error code (negative value).

See also: `gxSetDisplay, gxGetDisplay`

Example:

```
/*--------------------------------------------------------

Filename: gxSM.C

Function: gxSetMode

Description: Sets up the desired graphics or text mode

Prerequisite Function(s): gxSetDisplay

See PrintError() function described in Appendix A

--------------------------------------------------*/

#include <stdio.h>
#include <stdlib.h>
#include <conio.h>

#include <gxlib.h>
```

```
void PrintError(char * funcName, int retCode);

void
main()
{
    int retValue;        /* Return value storage    */
    int dispMode;        /* 640x480x16 color        */

    /* Local initialization section */

    dispMode = gxVGA_12; /* Set up 640x480x16 colors */
    retValue = 0;        /* Start clean              */


    /* Mandatory kernel initialization */

    retValue = gxSetDisplay(dispMode);
    if(retValue < 0)
    {
        PrintError("gxSetDisplay", retValue);
        return;
    }

    /*
       Note that the constant gxGRAPHICS is
       used, not the video mode number.
    */

    retValue = gxSetMode(gxGRAPHICS);
    if(retValue < 0)
    {
        PrintError("gxSetMode", retValue);
        return;
    }

    /* Wait for a user keypress, then clean up and exit */

    printf("Graphics mode enabled. Hit any key to
            exit... ");
    getch();

    /*
       In this case, the constant gxTEXT is used to
       get us back to the text mode we were in
       before this app fired up.
    */
```

```
retValue = gxSetMode(gxTEXT);
if(retValue < 0)
{
    PrintError("gxSetMode", retValue);
    return;
}

return;
}
```

GXSETPAGE

This function sets the current display page to the specified value. The first page is page zero.

Syntax: `int far pascal gxSetPage(page)`

Parameter: `page`

Type: `int`

Description: New page number to set.

Comments: The number of available display pages differs with each display type. You usually work with only one page—page zero. The list below shows the number of available pages for each display type that contains more than one page. The third column represents the possible argument to be used for this function.

Display Type	# of Pages	Page Range
gxEGA_D	8	0 to 7
gxEGA_E	4	0 to 3
gxEGA_F	2	0 to 1
gxEGA_10	2	0 to 1

Return value: Success returns `gxSUCCESS`. Failure returns an error code (negative value).

See also: `gxGetPage`

Example:

```
/* - - - - - - - - - - - - - - - - - - - - - - - - - - - - - - - - - - - - -
```

```
    Filename: gxSP.C

    Function: gxSetPage

    Description: Clears 2 display pages of 640x350x16,
                then swaps between them until a keypress

    Prerequisite Function(s): gxSetDisplay
                              gxSetMode
                              gxCreateVirtual
                              gxVirtualDisplay
                              gxDestroyVirtual


    See PrintError() function described in Appendix A

    - - - - - - - - - - - - - - - - - - - - - - - - - - - - - - - - - - - - - - - - - - - - - - - - - - - - - - */

    #include <stdio.h>
    #include <stdlib.h>
    #include <conio.h>

    #include <gxlib.h>

    void PrintError(char * funcName, int retCode);

    /* Global variables here... */


    void
    main()
    {
        int retValue;       /* Return value storage    */
        int dispMode;       /* 640x350x16 color        */

        /* Local initialization section */

        dispMode = gxEGA_10; /* Set up 640x350x16 colors */
        retValue = 0;        /* Start clean              */

        /* Mandatory kernel initialization */

        retValue = gxSetDisplay(dispMode);
        if(retValue < 0)
        {
```

```
    PrintError("gxSetDisplay", retValue);
    return;
}

/* Let's set up our desired video mode */

retValue = gxSetMode(gxGRAPHICS);
if(retValue < 0)
{
    PrintError("gxSetMode", retValue);
    return;
}

/* Clear page 0 to red */

retValue = gxClearDisplay(gxLIGHTRED, 0);

if(retValue < 0)
{
    PrintError("gxClearDisplay", retValue);
    return;
}

/* Clear page 1 to blue */

retValue = gxClearDisplay(gxLIGHTBLUE, 1);

if(retValue < 0)
{
    PrintError("gxClearDisplay", retValue);
    return;
}

/*
   Loop, toggling between pages at some reasonable
   rate, and continue until a keypress is sensed.
*/

while(!(kbhit()))
{
    gxSetPage(1);
    gxDelay(500);/* Delay 500/1000, or 1/2 second */

    gxSetPage(0);
    gxDelay(500);/* Delay 500/1000, or 1/2 second */
}
```

```
    getch();

    retValue = gxSetMode(gxTEXT);
    if(retValue < 0)
    {
        PrintError("gxSetMode", retValue);
        return;
    }

    return;
}
```

GXSETPALETTECOLOR

This function sets the specified palette index to the specified color value.

Syntax: `int far pascal gxSetPaletteColor(index, color)`

Parameter: `index`

Type: `int`

Description: Palette `index` value (0-15).

Parameter: `color`

Type: `int`

Description: New color to set.

Comments: This function sets the palette values for EGA modes only. Because the EGA mode contains only 16 colors, the `index` argument range is limited to 0 to 15. The `color` argument is limited in range from 0 to 63. The default color values are listed in Appendix A. See `gxSetPaletteRGB` to set the 16-color palette for VGA modes.

Return value: Success returns `gxSUCCESS`. Failure returns an error code (negative value).

See also: `gxSetPaletteRGB, gxGetPaletteColor`

Example:

```
/*--------------------------------------------------------

Filename: gxSPC.C

Function: gxSetPaletteColor

Description: Changes the color white in the palette
             to magenta, and prints it on the screen

Prerequisite Function(s): gxSetDisplay
                          gxSetMode

See PrintError() function described in Appendix A

--------------------------------------------------------*/

#include <stdio.h>
#include <stdlib.h>
#include <conio.h>

#include <gxlib.h>

void PrintError(char * funcName, int retCode);

void
main()
{
    int retValue;       /* Return value storage    */
    int dispMode;       /* 640x350x16 color        */
    int index;          /* Index counter           */

    /* Local initialization section */

    dispMode = gxEGA_10; /* Set up 640x350x16 colors */
    index    = 15;       /* Change index color 15    */
    retValue = 0;        /* Start clean              */

    /* Mandatory kernel initialization */

    retValue = gxSetDisplay(dispMode);
    if(retValue < 0)
    {
        PrintError("gxSetDisplay", retValue);
        return;
    }
```

```
/* Let's set up our desired video mode */

retValue = gxSetMode(gxGRAPHICS);
if(retValue < 0)
{
    PrintError("gxSetMode", retValue);
    return;
}

/*
   First, clear the display in the
   default color (white), and
   wait for a keypress
*/

retValue = gxClearDisplay(index, 0);
if(retValue < 0)
{
    PrintError("gxClearDisplay", retValue);
    return;
}

printf("\nHit any key to change this palette color
... ");
getch();

/*
   Here we change the palette index 15,
   which is currently white (63), to
   a magenta (5)
*/

retValue = gxSetPaletteColor(index, 5);
if(retValue < 0)
{
    PrintError("gxSetPaletteColor", retValue);
    return;
}

printf(" Done.\n");

getch();

/* Clean up and exit */

retValue = gxSetMode(gxTEXT);
if(retValue < 0)
```

```
    {
        PrintError("gxSetMode", retValue);
        return;
    }


    return;
}
```

GXSETPALETTERGB

This function sets the red, green, and blue component values for the desired palette index.

Syntax: `int far pascal gxSetPaletteRGB(index, red, green, blue)`

Parameter: `index`

Type: `int`

Description: Palette `index` value (0-255).

Parameter: `red`

Type: `int`

Description: New `red` component value.

Parameter: `green`

Type: `int`

Description: New `green` component value.

Parameter: `blue`

Type: `int`

Description: New `blue` component value.

Comments: This function sets the palette values for VGA modes only. Because there are 16 colors in the palette, the `index` argument range is limited to 0 to 15. Each color component argument has a range of 0 to 63. See `gxSetPaletteColor` to set palette colors for EGA modes.

Return value: Success returns `gxSUCCESS`. Failure returns an error code (negative value).

See also: `gxGetPaletteColor`, `gxDisplayPalette`, `gxGetDisplayInfo`

Example:

```
/*-----------------------------------------------------------

Filename: gxSPRGB.C

Function: gxSetPaletteRGB

Description: Changes the index 14 in the palette
             to magenta, and prints it on the screen
             in 640x480x16

Prerequisite Function(s): gxSetDisplay
                          gxSetMode
                          gxGetPaletteRGB

See PrintError() function described in Appendix A

-----------------------------------------------------------*/

#include <stdio.h>
#include <stdlib.h>
#include <conio.h>

#include <gxlib.h>

void PrintError(char * funcName, int retCode);

void
main()
{
    int retValue;        /* Return value storage   */
    int dispMode;        /* 640x480x16 color       */
    int index;           /* Index color            */
    int red, green, blue;/* Component colors        */
```

```
/* Local initialization section */

dispMode = gxVGA_12; /* Set up 640x480x16 color  */
index    = 14;       /* Change index color 14    */
retValue = 0;        /* Start clean              */

/* Mandatory kernel initialization */

retValue = gxSetDisplay(dispMode);
if(retValue < 0)
{
    PrintError("gxSetDisplay", retValue);
    return;
}

/* Let's set up our desired video mode */

retValue = gxSetMode(gxGRAPHICS);
if(retValue < 0)
{
    PrintError("gxSetMode", retValue);
    return;
}

/*
   First, save the current palette
   setting for restoring later
*/

retValue = gxGetPaletteRGB(index, &red, &green,
                                  &blue);
if(retValue < 0)
{
    PrintError("gxGetPaletteRGB", retValue);
    return;
}

/*
   Next, clear the display in the
   default color (yellow), and
   wait for a keypress
*/

retValue = gxClearDisplay(index, 0);
if(retValue < 0)
{
```

```
        PrintError("gxClearDisplay", retValue);
        return;
}

printf("\nHit any key to change this palette color ...
");
getch();

/*
   Here we change the palette index 14,
   which is currently yellow to
   a magenta (63,0,63)
*/

retValue = gxSetPaletteRGB(index, 63, 0, 63);
if(retValue < 0)
{
    PrintError("gxSetPaletteRGB", retValue);
    return;
}

printf(" Done.\n");
printf("Hit any key to change palette color
        back ... ");

getch();

/* Put palette value back to original (not required)*/

retValue = gxSetPaletteRGB(index, red, green, blue);
if(retValue < 0)
{
    PrintError("gxSetPaletteRGB", retValue);
    return;
}

printf(" Done.\n");

getch();

/* Clean up and exit */

retValue = gxSetMode(gxTEXT);
if(retValue < 0)
{
    PrintError("gxSetMode", retValue);
    return;
```

```
    }

    return;
}
```

GXSETRANDOM

This function sets to a specified value the seed for the random number generator.

Syntax: `int far pascal gxSetRandom(seed)`

Parameter: `seed`

Type: `int`

Description: New `seed` value.

Comments: Each time you start your application, the random number generator has the same seed, which produces the same pattern of random numbers. To generate a random series of random numbers every time your program runs, call this function at the start of your application using the time of day in seconds (or hundredths of seconds) as the seed. This ensures a random seed and a random number series. The range for `seed` is from 0 to 32,000.

Return value: Success returns `gxSUCCESS`. Failure returns an error code (negative value).

See also: `gxGetRandom`

Example:

```
/*--------------------------------------------------------

Filename: gxSR.C

Function: gxSetRandom

Description: Sets the seed for the random number genera-
            tor to the current time of day in seconds,
            then prints out a set of random numbers
```

```
Prerequisite Function(s): gxSetDisplay
                          gxGetRandom

See PrintError() function described in Appendix A

-------------------------------------------------------*/

#include <stdio.h>
#include <stdlib.h>
#include <conio.h>
#include <dos.h>

#include <gxlib.h>

void PrintError(char * funcName, int retCode);
int TimeOfDay(void);

void
main()
{
    int retValue;       /* Return value storage       */
    int dispMode;       /* 640x480x16 color           */
    int range;          /* random maximum value       */
    int cnt;            /* random numbers loop        */

    /* Local initialization section */

    dispMode = gxVGA_12; /* Set up 640x480x16 colors */
    range    = 256;      /* random must be < 256     */
    cnt      = 0;        /* General purpose counter  */
    retValue = 0;        /* start clean              */

    /* Mandatory kernel initialization */

    retValue = gxSetDisplay(dispMode);
    if(retValue < 0)
    {
        PrintError("gxSetDisplay", retValue);
        return;
    }

    /* Start the random series at a random time */

    retValue = gxSetRandom(TimeOfDay());
    if(retValue < 0)
```

```
    {
        PrintError("gxSetRandom", retValue);
        return;
    }

    /*
        Display the first five random numbers in the
        series. We have requested the range of 0 to 255.
    */

    for(cnt=0; cnt<5; cnt++)
    {
        retValue = gxGetRandom(range);
        if(retValue < 0)
        {
            PrintError("gxGetRandom", retValue);
            return;
        }
        printf("Random number is %d\n", retValue);
    }

    return;
}

/**********/

/*
 * A short function to get us a random seed number
 * from the time of day.
 *
 */

int
TimeOfDay()
{
    union REGS inregs, outregs;

    inregs.h.ah = 0x2c;
    int86(0x21, &inregs, &outregs);
    return(((outregs.h.dl * outregs.h.dh) +
outregs.h.dl));
}
```

GXVERIFYDISPLAYTYPE

This function verifies whether a given display type can be used (i.e., is supported) on the current video hardware.

Syntax: `int far pascal gxVerifyDisplayType(dType)`

Parameter: `dType`

Type: `int`

Description: Display type to verify.

Comments: This function is useful when you want to determine if the user has the correct hardware to run your program. You can also use `gxVideoInfo` to determine the exact hardware configuration.

Return value: Success returns `gxSUCCESS`. Failure returns an error code (negative value).

See also: `gxSetDisplay`, `gxGetDisplay`, `gxVideoInfo`

Example:

```
/*-------------------------------------------------------

Filename: gxVDT.C

Function: gxVerifyDisplayType

Description: Verifies the current video hardware sup-
            ports VGA 640x480x16 color

Prerequisite Function(s): gxSetDisplay

See PrintError() function described in Appendix A

-----------------------------------------------------*/

#include <stdio.h>
#include <stdlib.h>
#include <conio.h>

#include <gxlib.h>
```

```
void PrintError(char * funcName, int retCode);

void
main()
{
    int retValue;         /* Return value storage    */
    int dispMode;         /* 640x480x16 color        */

    /* Local initialization section */

    dispMode = gxVGA_12;  /* Set up 640x480x16 colors */
    retValue = 0;         /* Start clean               */

    /* Mandatory kernel initialization */

    retValue = gxSetDisplay(dispMode);
    if(retValue < 0)
    {
        PrintError("gxSetDisplay", retValue);
        return;
    }

    /* Does the current hardware support desired mode?*/

    retValue = gxVerifyDisplayType(dispMode);
    if(retValue < 0)
    {
        PrintError("gxVerifyDisplayType", retValue);
        return;
    }
    else
    {
        printf("The current hardware supports VGA ");
        printf("640x480x16 color mode 12H\n");
    }

    return;
}
```

GXVIDEOINFO

This function returns display adapter configuration information. It returns information on up to two display adapter/monitor combinations.

Syntax: `int far pascal gxVideoInfo(vi)`

Parameter: `vi`

Type: `GXVINFO` *

Description: Location to store two video information structures.

Comments: This function expects the argument pointer to be allocated to store two `GXVINFO` structures (for example, `GXVINFO vi[2];`). If you don't have the proper memory allocated, you will overwrite your program! The following list shows defined adapter and monitor types:

Adapter Constant	Value	Type of Display Adapter
`viNONE`	0	No adapter found
`viMDA`	1	Monochrome display adapter
`viCGA`	2	Color graphics adapter
`viEGA`	3	Enhanced graphics adapter
`viMCGA`	4	Multicolor graphics adapter
`viVGA`	5	Video graphics array
`viHGC`	80 hex	Hercules Graphics Card
`viHGCPlus`	81 hex	Hercules Graphics Card Plus
`viHGCColor`	82 hex	Hercules InColor Card

Display Constants	Value	Type of Monitor
`viMDAdisp`	1	Monochrome display monitor
`viCGAdisp`	2	Color graphics display monitor
`viEGAdisp`	3	Enhanced graphics display monitor
`viVGAmono`	4	VGA monochrome display monitor
`viVGAcolor`	5	VGA color display monitor

Return value: Success returns gxSUCCESS. Failure returns an error code (negative value).

See also: gxSetDisplay, gxGetDisplay

Example:

```
/*----------------------------------------------------

Filename: gxVI.C

Function: gxVideoInfo

Description: Returns the PC display information into
            the structure array VI

Prerequisite Function(s): gxSetDisplay

See PrintError() function described in Appendix A

---------------------------------------------------*/

#include <stdio.h>
#include <stdlib.h>
#include <conio.h>

#include <gxlib.h>

void PrintError(char * funcName, int retCode);

/* Global variables here... */

GXVINFO vidInfo[2];            /* 2 structures are re-
quired */

char * viadapt[] = {"[None]","MDA","CGA","EGA",
                    "MCGA","VGA"};
char * vidisp [] = {"[None]","MDA Mono Display",
                    "CGA Color Display","EGA Color
                    Display", "VGA Mono Display","VGA
                    Color Display"};
char * viherc [] = {"HGC","HGC+","InColor"};

void
main()
{
```

```c
int retValue;        /* Return value storage    */
int dispMode;        /* 640x480x16 color        */
int i;               /* Index counter           */

/* Local initialization section */

dispMode = gxVGA_12; /* Set up 640x480x16 colors */
retValue = 0;        /* Start clean             */

/* Mandatory kernel initialization */

retValue = gxSetDisplay(dispMode);
if(retValue < 0)
{
    PrintError("gxSetDisplay", retValue);
    return;
}

/* Get the current display type */

retValue = gxVideoInfo(vidInfo);
if(retValue < 0)
{
    PrintError("gxVideoInfo", retValue);
    return;
}

/*
   Print the information, wait for a keypress,
   then exit
*/

printf("\ngxVideoInfo returned:\n\n");

/* Display what we found */
for (i=0; i<=1; i++) {

  /* Is there an adapter here? */
  if (vidInfo[i].adapter != viNONE) {

    /* Display, and use the other array if Hercules*/
    if (vidInfo[i].adapter >= viHGC)
    {
      printf("  %-7s with a %s\n",
              viherc[vidInfo[i].adapter-viHGC],
              vidisp[vidInfo[i].display]);
```

```
    }
    else
    {
      printf("  %-7s with a %s\n",
             viadapt[vidInfo[i].adapter],
             vidisp[vidInfo[i].display]);
    }
  }
}

printf("\n");

return;
}
```

GXVIRTUALDISPLAY

This function places onto the display part or all of an image located in a virtual buffer. The gxVirtualDisplay function is similar to gxPutImage, except that this function enables you to specify the virtual buffer coordinates at which you wish to start displaying. With this function, you can easily create such graphics as custom windows and scroll routines.

Syntax: int far pascal gxVirtualDisplay(vhPtr, vx, vy, x1, y1, x2, y2, page)

Parameter: vhPtr

Type: GXHEADER *

Description: Pointer to GXHEADER structure.

Parameter: vx,vy

Type: int

Description: x and y pixel offset into virtual image to begin displaying.

Parameter: x1,y1

Type: int

Description: Upper-left corner of display in which to place image window.

Parameter: x2,y2

Type: int

Description: Lower-right corner of display in which to place image window.

Parameter: page

Type: int

Description: Page on which to place image.

Comments: You must first place an image into vhPtr by calling gxGetImage or by some other means. See Appendix A for a listing of the GXHEADER structures. The display coordinates x1,y1 and x2,y2 define the size of the display area (window) where the image is displayed. The first image line displayed is defined by the vx,vy coordinate pair.

Return value: Success returns gxSUCCESS. Failure returns an error code (negative value).

See also: gxCreateVirtual, gxGetImage, gxPutImage

Example:

```
/*-------------------------------------------------------

Filename: gxVD.C

Function: gxVirtualDisplay
```

```
Description: Creates 2 virtual buffers, one blue, one
             green and displays them both on the screen
             one at a time

Prerequisite Function(s): gxSetDisplay
                          gxSetMode
                          gxCreateVirtual
                          gxDestoryVirtual


See PrintError() function described in Appendix A

-----------------------------------------------------*/

#include <stdio.h>
#include <stdlib.h>
#include <conio.h>

#include <gxlib.h>

void PrintError(char * funcName, int retCode);

/* Global variables here... */

GXHEADER vHeader[2];      /* Storage for virtual bufs */

void
main()
{
    int retValue;         /* Return value storage      */
    int dispMode;         /* 640x480x16 color          */

    /* Local initialization section */

    dispMode = gxVGA_12; /* Set up 640x480x16 colors */
    retValue = 0;         /* Start clean               */

    /* Mandatory kernel initialization */

    retValue = gxSetDisplay(dispMode);
    if(retValue < 0)
    {
        PrintError("gxSetDisplay", retValue);
        return;
    }
```

```
/* Let's set up our desired video mode */

retValue = gxSetMode(gxGRAPHICS);
if(retValue < 0)
{
    PrintError("gxSetMode", retValue);
    return;
}

/*
   Create the first of 2 virtual buffers
   in conventional memory that is
   640 by 480 in pixels
*/

retValue = gxCreateVirtual(gxCMM, &vHeader[0],
                            dispMode, 640, 480);
if(retValue < 0)
{
    PrintError("gxCreateVirtual", retValue);
    return;
}

/*
   Create the second of 2 virtual buffers
   in conventional memory that is
   640 by 480 in pixels
*/

retValue = gxCreateVirtual(gxCMM, &vHeader[1],
                            dispMode, 640, 480);
if(retValue < 0)
{
    PrintError("gxCreateVirtual", retValue);
    return;
}

/*
   Once created, the virtual buffer is all
   zeros (black). Clear #1 to green first.
*/

retValue = gxClearVirtual(&vHeader[0], gxGREEN);
if(retValue < 0)
{
```

```
      PrintError("gxClearVirtual", retValue);
      return;
}

retValue = gxClearVirtual(&vHeader[1], gxBLUE);
if(retValue < 0)
{
    PrintError("gxClearVirtual", retValue);
    return;
}

/*
   Print the green buffer onto the display.
   The first set of zeros are the virtual
   offset x and y.  The second and third
   set of coordinates are the screen
   beginning and ending coordinates.
*/

retValue = gxVirtualDisplay(&vHeader[0],
                      0,0, 0,0, 639,479, 0);
if(retValue < 0)
{
    PrintError("gxVirtualDisplay", retValue);
    return;
}

/* Wait for the first user keypress */

getch();

/*
   Print the blue buffer onto the display.
   The first set of zeros are the virtual
   offset x and y.  The second and third
   set of coordinates are the screen
   beginning and ending coordinates.
*/

retValue = gxVirtualDisplay(&vHeader[1],
                      0,0, 0,0, 639,479, 1);
if(retValue < 0)
{
    PrintError("gxVirtualDisplay", retValue);
    return;
}
```

```
getch();

/* Deallocate both virtual blocks */

retValue = gxDestroyVirtual(&vHeader[0]);
if(retValue < 0)
{
    PrintError("gxDestroyVirtual", retValue);
    return;
}

retValue = gxDestroyVirtual(&vHeader[1]);
if(retValue < 0)
{
    PrintError("gxDestroyVirtual", retValue);
    return;
}

retValue = gxSetMode(gxTEXT);
if(retValue < 0)
{
    PrintError("gxSetMode", retValue);
    return;
}

return;
}
```

GXVIRTUALFREE

This function determines the amount of free memory available for virtual buffers. This memory is conventional memory.

Syntax: `long far pascal gxVirtualFree(vType)`

Parameter: vType

Type: int

Description: Type of memory to check.

Comments: This function returns the amount of free memory to a long integer; it doesn't return an error code. See gxCreateVirtual for a listing of values to set vType.

Return value: The amount of available memory in bytes.

See also: gxCreateVirtual, gxDestroyVirtual

Example:

```
/*-------------------------------------------------------

Filename: gxVF.C

Function: gxVirtualFree

Description: Finds the amount of conventional memory
            left

Prerequisite Function(s): gxSetDisplay
                          gxSetMode

See PrintError() function described in Appendix A

-----------------------------------------------------*/

#include <stdio.h>
#include <stdlib.h>
#include <conio.h>

#include <gxlib.h>

void PrintError(char * funcName, int retCode);

void
main()
{
    int retValue;        /* Return value storage   */
    int dispMode;        /* 640x480x16 color       */
    long memFree;        /* Storage for free mem cnt */

    /* Local initialization section */

    dispMode = gxVGA_12; /* Set up 640x480x16 colors */
    retValue = 0;        /* Start clean             */

    /* Mandatory kernel initialization */

    retValue = gxSetDisplay(dispMode);
    if(retValue < 0)
    {
```

```
        PrintError("gxSetDisplay", retValue);
        return;
    }

    memFree = gxVirtualFree(gxCMM);
    printf("There are %ld bytes of memory
available.\n\n",
            memFree);

    return;
}
```

GXVIRTUALSIZE

This function calculates the number of bytes of virtual buffer memory required to store an image of a specified width, height, and pixel depth.

Syntax: `long far pascal gxVirtualSize(dType, width, height)`

Parameter: `dType`

Type: `int`

Description: Display type.

Parameter: `width`

Type: `int`

Description: Width of buffer in pixels.

Parameter: `height`

Type: `int`

Description: Height of buffer in pixels.

Comments: This function is most useful if you allocate memory yourself (instead of using `gxCreateVirtual`) or if you need to know the size requirements beforehand. See `gxSetDisplay` for a listing of valid values for `dType`.

Return value: The amount in bytes of memory required for the buffer.

See also: gxCreateVirtual, gxDestroyVirtual

Example:

```
/*------------------------------------------------------------

Filename: gxVS.C

Function: gxVirtualSize

Description: Finds the amount of memory necessary to
            store a 640x480x16 color image

Prerequisite Function(s): gxSetDisplay
                          gxSetMode

See PrintError() function described in Appendix A

----------------------------------------------------*/

#include <stdio.h>
#include <stdlib.h>
#include <conio.h>

#include <gxlib.h>

void PrintError(char * funcName, int retCode);

void
main()
{
    int retValue;       /* Return value storage    */
    int dispMode;       /* 640x480x16 color        */
    long memSize;       /* Storage for free mem cnt */

    /* Local initialization section */

    dispMode = gxVGA_12; /* Set up 640x480x16 colors */
    retValue = 0;        /* Start clean              */
```

```
/* Mandatory kernel initialization */

retValue = gxSetDisplay(dispMode);
if(retValue < 0)
{
    PrintError("gxSetDisplay", retValue);
    return;
}

memSize = gxVirtualSize(dispMode, 640, 480);
printf("For an image of 640x480x16, ");
printf("%ld bytes of memory are
required.\n\n",memSize);

    return;
}
```

INTRODUCTION TO MAJOR GRAPHICS FUNCTIONS

This chapter describes the PowerPack major graphics functions, which, as the title suggests, make up most of the graphics routines. Text drawing also is in the graphics functions. Several functions in this chapter mention predefined structures and data types found in the header file GRLIB.H and Appendix A. To get these functions, add the GRLIB.H file to each source file that calls these routines and add the GR_CL.LIB file (for large memory model) to your link list.

All examples in this chapter are complete, executable functions that were compiled in the small memory model. The only missing source code piece is the PrintError function, which is listed in Appendix A. Some functions rely on others to operate; they are noted as such. In each example, the specific function being described is displayed in bold type.

GRCLEARVIEWPORT

This function clears the currently defined viewport with the current background color.

Syntax: int far pascal grClearViewPort(void)

Parameter: None.

Comments: The viewport can act as a window, allowing drawing functions to take place with respect to the viewport coordinates, without concern for the exact screen coordinates. You must call the function grSetViewPort to set up viewport coordinates before you can clear the viewport. Retrieve the current background color with a call to the function grGetBkColor and set with a call to grSetBkColor.

Return value: Success returns gxSUCCESS. Failure returns an error code (negative value).

See also: grGetViewPort, grSetViewPort, grGetBkColor, grSetBkColor

Example:
```
/*-------------------------------------------------------

Filename: grCVP.C

Function: grClearViewPort

Description: Sets the current viewport coordinates
            to the lower-right quadrant of the screen,
            draws a hatch pattern at 0,0 of the
            viewport coordinates, and clears it
```

```
Prerequisite Function(s): gxSetDisplay
                          gxSetMode
                          grSetFillStyle
                          grDrawRect
                          grSetViewPort

See PrintError() function described in Appendix A

---------------------------------------------------------*/

#include <stdio.h>
#include <stdlib.h>
#include <conio.h>

#include <gxlib.h>
#include <grlib.h>

void PrintError(char * funcName, int retCode);

void
main()
{
    int retValue;       /* Return value storage    */
    int dispMode;       /* 640x480x16 color        */
    int dispColor;      /* Display Color           */
    int dispPage;       /* Display Page            */

    /* Local initialization section */

    dispMode = gxVGA_12;    /* Set up 640x480x16 colors */
    dispColor = gxRED;      /* Do a full red screen     */
    dispPage = 0;           /* Page 0                   */
    retValue = 0;           /* Start clean              */

    /* Mandatory kernel initialization */

    retValue = gxSetDisplay(dispMode);
    if(retValue < 0)
    {
        PrintError("gxSetDisplay", retValue);
        return;
    }

    /* Let's set up our desired video mode */
```

```
retValue = gxSetMode(gxGRAPHICS);
if(retValue < 0)
{
    PrintError("gxSetMode", retValue);
    return;
}

/*
   The fill style and color must be set
   before doing a grDrawRect
*/

retValue = grSetFillStyle(grFTHHATCH, grCYAN,
                          grOPAQUE);
if(retValue < 0)
{
    PrintError("grSetFillStyle", retValue);
    return;
}

/*
   Set the viewport coordinates to be at
   the lower-right quadrant of screen
*/

retValue = grSetViewPort(320,240, 639,479);
if(retValue < 0)
{
    PrintError("grSetViewPort", retValue);
    return;
}

/*
   Draw a rectangle (which will be a
   hatch pattern in red) at viewport
   coordinates 0,0
*/

retValue = grDrawRect(0,0, 319,239, grFILL);
if(retValue < 0)
{
    PrintError("grDrawRect", retValue);
    return;
}

/* wait for a user keypress */
```

```
getch();

/* Set the background color */

retValue = grSetBkColor(gxLIGHTBLUE);
if(retValue < 0)
{
    PrintError("grDrawRect", retValue);
    return;
}

/* Clear the viewport */

retValue = grClearViewPort();
if(retValue < 0)
{
    PrintError("grClearViewPort", retValue);
    return;
}

/* wait for a user keypress, then clearup and exit */

getch();

retValue = gxSetMode(gxTEXT);
if(retValue < 0)
{
    PrintError("gxSetMode", retValue);
    return;
}

return;
}
```

GRDEFAULTSTATE

This function resets the graphics state to its default drawing color, line, fill styles, and so forth.

Syntax: `int far pascal grDefaultState(void)`

Parameter: None.

Comments: The default state is described in the following list.

Graphics Function	State
Active Page	0
Drawing Color	grBLUE
Background Color	grBLACK
Current Position (CP)	(0,0)
Logical Operation	gxSET
Clipping	gxFALSE
Fill Style	grFSOLID
Fill Color	grBLACK
Fill Transparency	grTRANS
Line Style	grLSOLID
Line Thickness	1
Viewport	(0,0) to (1023,1023)
Text Style	grTXT8X8
Text Transparency	grTRANS
Text Justification	(grLEFT, grTOP)

Return value: Success returns gxSUCCESS. Failure returns an error code (negative value).

See also: grGetState, grSetState

Example:

```
/*-------------------------------------------------------

Filename: grDS.C

Function: grDefaultState

Description: Resets the current drawing color, line
            size, fill style, etc. back to the startup
            values;This function doesn't do anything
            fun.

Prerequisite Function(s): gxSetDisplay

See PrintError() function described in Appendix A

-----------------------------------------------------*/
```

```c
#include <stdio.h>
#include <stdlib.h>
#include <conio.h>

#include <gxlib.h>
#include <grlib.h>

void PrintError(char * funcName, int retCode);

void
main()
{
    int retValue;        /* Return value storage    */
    int dispMode;        /* 640x480x16 color        */

    /* Local initialization section */

    dispMode = gxVGA_12;  /* Set up 640x480x16 colors */
    retValue = 0;         /* Start clean               */

    /* Mandatory kernel initialization */

    retValue = gxSetDisplay(dispMode);
    if(retValue < 0)
    {
        PrintError("gxSetDisplay", retValue);
        return;
    }

    retValue = grDefaultState();
    if(retValue < 0)
    {
        PrintError("grDefaultState", retValue);
        return;
    }
    else
    {
        printf("State has been returned to \
                defaults.\n");
    }

    return;
}
```

GRDISPLAYMOUSE

This function enables or disables display of the mouse cursor.

Syntax: `int far pascal grDisplayMouse(dFlag)`

Parameter: `dFlag`

Type: `int`

Description: `grSHOW` or `grHIDE`.

Comments: If `dFlag` is set to `grSHOW`, the mouse is displayed. If `dFlag` is set to `grHIDE`, the mouse is hidden. Actually, the mouse driver keeps an internal counter (much like the Microsoft mouse). This counter decrements at each function call with `grHIDE` and increments at each call with `grSHOW`. Therefore, the same number of calls with `grSHOW` must replace the successive calls with `grHIDE`. Note that the mouse driver must first be initialized with a call to the function `grInitMouse`. See the function `grTrackMouse` to force the PowerPack to move the mouse cursor. You should always hide the mouse when drawing graphics or text on the display.

Return value: Success returns `gxSUCCESS`. Failure returns an error code (negative value).

See also: `grInitMouse`

Example:

```
/* - - - - - - - - - - - - - - - - - - - - - - - - - - - - - - - - - - - - - - - - - - - - - - - - -

Filename: grDM.C

Function: grDisplayMouse

Description: Displays the mouse; then turns it off after
            a keypress

Prerequisite Function(s): gxSetDisplay
                          gxSetMode
                          grInitMouse
                          grTrackMouse
                          grStopMouse
```

See PrintError() function described in Appendix A

```
- - - - - - - - - - - - - - - - - - - - - - - - - - - - - - - - - - - - - - - - - - - -*/

#include <stdio.h>
#include <stdlib.h>
#include <conio.h>

#include <gxlib.h>
#include <grlib.h>

void PrintError(char * funcName, int retCode);

void
main()
{
    int retValue;          /* Return value storage   */
    int dispMode;          /* 640x480x16 color       */

    /* Local initialization section */

    dispMode = gxVGA_12;   /* Set up 640x480x16 colors */
    retValue = 0;          /* Start clean             */

    /* Mandatory kernel initialization */

    retValue = gxSetDisplay(dispMode);
    if(retValue < 0)
    {
        PrintError("gxSetDisplay", retValue);
        return;
    }

    /* Let's set up our desired video mode */

    retValue = gxSetMode(gxGRAPHICS);
    if(retValue < 0)
    {
        PrintError("gxSetMode", retValue);
        return;
    }

    /* Initialize and install mouse driver */
```

```
retValue = grInitMouse();
if(retValue < 0)
{
    PrintError("grInitMouse", retValue);
    return;
}

/* Track the mouse movement */

retValue = grTrackMouse(grTRACK);
if(retValue < 0)
{
    PrintError("grTrackMouse", retValue);
    return;
}

/* Turn the mouse on */

retValue = grDisplayMouse(grSHOW);
if(retValue < 0)
{
    PrintError("grDisplayMouse", retValue);
    return;
}

/* Wait for a user keypress */

getch();

/* Turn the mouse off */

retValue = grDisplayMouse(grHIDE);
if(retValue < 0)
{
    PrintError("grDisplayMouse", retValue);
    return;
}

/* De-init and remove mouse driver */

retValue = grStopMouse();
if(retValue < 0)
{
    PrintError("grStopMouse", retValue);
```

```
        return;
    }

    /* Return to text mode */

    retValue = gxSetMode(gxTEXT);
    if(retValue < 0)
    {
        PrintError("gxSetMode", retValue);
        return;
    }

    return;
}
```

GRDRAWCIRCLE

This function draws a circle, centered at the specified coordinates.

Syntax: `int far pascal grDrawCircle(x, y, radius, fillFlag)`

Parameter: `x, y`

Type: `int`

Description: Coordinates at which a circle is center-displayed.

Parameter: `radius`

Type: `int`

Description: Radius of a circle.

Parameter: `fillFlag`

Type: `int`

Description: `grOUTLINE` and/or `grFILL`.

Comments: The circle is drawn with the center at the specified coordinates. The `fillFlag` argument specifies whether the circle outline is drawn with the current drawing color (`grOUTLINE`), filled

with the current fill color and fill style (grFILL), or both outlined
and filled (grOUTPUT + grFILL). Note that only the fill style affects
the drawing of circles and ellipses—line styles do not affect that.
The table displayed in the function page for grDrawRect shows the
five main draw/fill routines and the three routines that affect color
and style. Check that table for the color and style routine you need
for grDrawCircle.

Return value: Success returns gxSUCCESS. Failure returns an error
code (negative value).

See also: grGetFillStyle, grSetFillStyle, grGetColor, grSetColor

Example:

```
/*-----------------------------------------------------------

Filename: grDC.C

Function: grDrawCircle

Description: Draws a yellow circle in the middle of the
            screen

Prerequisite Function(s): gxSetDisplay
                          gxSetMode
                          grSetFillStyle

See PrintError() function described in Appendix A

----------------------------------------------------------*/

#include <stdio.h>
#include <stdlib.h>
#include <conio.h>

#include <gxlib.h>
#include <grlib.h>

void PrintError(char * funcName, int retCode);

void
main()
{
    int retValue;            /* Return value storage    */
```

```
int dispMode;          /* 640x480x16 color         */

/* Local initialization section */

dispMode = gxVGA_12;   /* Set up 640x480x16 colors */
retValue = 0;          /* Start clean              */

/* Mandatory kernel initialization */

retValue = gxSetDisplay(dispMode);
if(retValue < 0)
{
    PrintError("gxSetDisplay", retValue);
    return;
}

/* Let's set up our desired video mode */

retValue = gxSetMode(gxGRAPHICS);
if(retValue < 0)
{
    PrintError("gxSetMode", retValue);
    return;
}

/*
   The fill style and color must be set
   before doing a grDrawRect
*/

retValue = grSetFillStyle(grFSOLID, grYELLOW,
            grOPAQUE);
if(retValue < 0)
{
    PrintError("grSetFillStyle", retValue);
    return;
}

/*
   Draw a circle (which will be a
   solid pattern) in yellow with a
   blue (default outline color) outline
*/
```

```
retValue = grDrawCircle(320,240, 50,
            grOUTLINE+grFILL);
if(retValue < 0)
{
    PrintError("grDrawCircle", retValue);
    return;
}

/* wait for a user keypress, then clean up and exit */

getch();

retValue = gxSetMode(gxTEXT);
if(retValue < 0)
{
    PrintError("gxSetMode", retValue);
    return;
}

return;
}
```

GRDRAWELLIPSE

This function draws an ellipse, centered at the specified coordinates.

Syntax: `int far pascal grDrawEllipse(x, y, width, height, fillFlag)`

Parameter: x, y

Type: `int`

Description: Coordinates at which an ellipse is center-displayed.

Parameter: `width, height`

Type: `int`

Description: Width and height of an ellipse in pixels, respectively.

Parameter: `fillFlag`

Topic: `int`

Description: `grOUTLINE` and/or `grFILL`.

Comments: The ellipse, with height as `height` and width as `width`, is drawn with the center at specified coordinates. The `fillFlag` argument indicates whether the ellipse outline is drawn with the current drawing color (`grOUTLINE`), filled with the current fill color and fill style (`grFILL`), or both outlined and filled (`grOUTPUT` + `grFILL`). Note that only the fill style affects drawing circles and ellipses—line styles do not affect that. The table displayed in the function page for `grDrawRect` shows the five main draw/fill routines and the three routines affecting color and style. Check that table for the color and style routine you need for `grDrawEllipse`.

Return value: Success returns `gxSUCCESS`. Failure returns an error code (negative value).

See also: `grGetFillStyle, grSetFillStyle, grGetColor, grSetColor`

Example:

```
/*- - - - - - - - - - - - - - - - - - - - - - - - - - - - - - - - - - - - - -

Filename: grDE.C

Function: grDrawEllipse

Description: Draws a magenta ellipse in the middle of
            the screen

Prerequisite Function(s): gxSetDisplay
                          gxSetMode
                          grSetFillStyle

See PrintError() function described in Appendix A

- - - - - - - - - - - - - - - - - - - - - - - - - - - - - - - - - - - - -*/

#include <stdio.h>
#include <stdlib.h>
```

```c
#include <conio.h>

#include <gxlib.h>
#include <grlib.h>

void PrintError(char * funcName, int retCode);

void
main()
{
    int retValue;        /* Return value storage    */
    int dispMode;        /* 640x480x16 color        */

    /* Local initialization section */

    dispMode = gxVGA_12;  /* Set up 640x480x16 colors */
    retValue = 0;         /* Start clean               */

    /* Mandatory kernel initialization */

    retValue = gxSetDisplay(dispMode);
    if(retValue < 0)
    {
        PrintError("gxSetDisplay", retValue);
        return;
    }

    /* Let's set up our desired video mode */

    retValue = gxSetMode(gxGRAPHICS);
    if(retValue < 0)
    {
        PrintError("gxSetMode", retValue);
        return;
    }

    /*
        The fill style and color must be set
        before doing a grDrawRect
    */

    retValue = grSetFillStyle(grFSOLID, grMAGENTA,
                grOPAQUE);
```

```
if(retValue < 0)
{
    PrintError("grSetFillStyle", retValue);
    return;
}

/*
    Draw an ellipse (which will be a
    solid pattern) in magenta with
    no outline
*/

retValue = grDrawEllipse(320,240, 100,50, grFILL);
if(retValue < 0)
{
    PrintError("grDrawEllipse", retValue);
    return;
}

/* wait for a user keypress, then clean up and exit */

getch();

retValue = gxSetMode(gxTEXT);
if(retValue < 0)
{
    PrintError("gxSetMode", retValue);
    return;
}

    return;
}
```

GRDRAWLINE

This function draws a line of the current line style and thickness at specified coordinates.

Syntax: `int far pascal grDrawLine(x1, y1, x2, y2)`

Parameter: x1, y1

Type: `int`

Description: Start-of-line coordinates.

Parameter: x2, y2

Type: int

Description: End-of-line coordinates.

Comments: The line is drawn with the current style and thickness, from the x1,y1 coordinate pair to the x2,y2 coordinate pair. The table on the function page for grDrawRect shows the five main draw/fill routines and the three routines that affect color and style. Check that table for the color and style routine you need for grDrawLine.

Return value: Success returns gxSUCCESS. Failure returns an error code (negative value).

See also: grGetLineStyle, grSetLineStyle, grGetColor, grSetColor

Example:

```
/*-----------------------------------------------------------

Filename: grDL.C

Function: grDrawLine

Description: Draws a magenta vertical line in the middle
            of the screen

Prerequisite Function(s): gxSetDisplay
                          gxSetMode
                          grSetColor

See PrintError() function described in Appendix A

-----------------------------------------------------*/

#include <stdio.h>
#include <stdlib.h>
#include <conio.h>

#include <gxlib.h>
#include <grlib.h>

void PrintError(char * funcName, int retCode);
```

```c
void
main()
{
    int retValue;          /* Return value storage    */
    int dispMode;          /* 640x480x16 color        */

    /* Local initialization section */

    dispMode = gxVGA_12;   /* Set up 640x480x16 colors */
    retValue = 0;          /* Start clean              */

    /* Mandatory kernel initialization */

    retValue = gxSetDisplay(dispMode);
    if(retValue < 0)
    {
        PrintError("gxSetDisplay", retValue);
        return;
    }

    /* Let's set up our desired video mode */

    retValue = gxSetMode(gxGRAPHICS);
    if(retValue < 0)
    {
        PrintError("gxSetMode", retValue);
        return;
    }

    /* Let's set the line color */

    retValue = grSetColor(grMAGENTA);
    if(retValue < 0)
    {
        PrintError("grSetColor", retValue);
        return;
    }

    /* Draw a line in magenta */

    retValue = grDrawLine(320,0, 320, 479);
    if(retValue < 0)
    {
        PrintError("grDrawLine", retValue);
        return;
    }
```

```
/* wait for a user keypress, then clean up and exit */

getch();

retValue = gxSetMode(gxTEXT);
if(retValue < 0)
{
    PrintError("gxSetMode", retValue);
    return;
}

return;
}
```

GRDRAWRECT

This function draws a rectangle at the specified boundary coordinates.

Syntax: `int far pascal grDrawRect(x1, y1, x2, y2, fillFlag)`

Parameter: x1, y1

Type: `int`

Description: Upper-left corner of rectangle.

Parameter: x2, y2

Type: `int`

Description: Lower-right corner of rectangle.

Parameter: `fillFlag`

Type: `int`

Description: `grOUTLINE` and/or `grFILL`

Comments: The rectangle is drawn at specified coordinate boundaries using the current line style and thickness and the current foreground color and fill style. The following list shows the five main draw/fill routines and the three routines affecting color and style. Check this list to see which color and style routine you need for grDrawRect.

Draw Function	grSetColor	grSetFillStyle	grSetLineStyle
grDrawRect	Outline Color	Fill Color	Outline Style
grDrawCircle	Outline Color	Fill Color	Outline Style
grDrawSquare	Outline Color	Fill Color	Outline Style
grDrawEllipse	Outline Color	Fill Color	Outline Style
grDrawLine	Line Color	N/A	Line Style

Return value: Success returns gxSUCCESS. Failure returns an error code (negative value).

See also: grGetLineStyle, grSetLineStyle, grGetColor, grSetColor, grGetFillStyle, grSetFillStyle

Example:

```
/*-------------------------------------------------------

Filename: grDR.C

Function: grDrawRect

Description: Draws a red rectangle with a green border
             at 0,0 on the screen

Prerequisite Function(s): gxSetDisplay
                          gxSetMode
                          grSetColor
                          grSetFillStyle

See PrintError() function described in Appendix A

-------------------------------------------------------*/

#include <stdio.h>
#include <stdlib.h>
#include <conio.h>
```

```c
#include <gxlib.h>
#include <grlib.h>

void PrintError(char * funcName, int retCode);

void
main()
{
    int retValue;       /* Return value storage    */
    int dispMode;       /* 640x480x16 color        */

    /* Local initialization section */

    dispMode = gxVGA_12;  /* Set up 640x480x16 colors */
    retValue = 0;         /* Start clean              */

    /* Mandatory kernel initialization */

    retValue = gxSetDisplay(dispMode);
    if(retValue < 0)
    {
        PrintError("gxSetDisplay", retValue);
        return;
    }

    /* Let's set up our desired video mode */

    retValue = gxSetMode(gxGRAPHICS);
    if(retValue < 0)
    {
        PrintError("gxSetMode", retValue);
        return;
    }

    /* Let's make the outline color green */

    retValue = grSetColor(gxGREEN);
    if(retValue < 0)
    {
        PrintError("grSetColor", retValue);
        return;
    }

    /*
        The fill style and color must be set
        before doing a grDrawRect
    */
```

```
retValue = grSetFillStyle(grFHATCH, grRED,
            grOPAQUE);
if(retValue < 0)
{
    PrintError("grSetFillStyle", retValue);
    return;
}

/*
   Draw a rectangle (which will be a
   hatch pattern in red) at screen
   coordinates 0,0
*/

retValue = grDrawRect(0,0, 75,100,
            grFILL+grOUTLINE);
if(retValue < 0)
{
    PrintError("grDrawRect", retValue);
    return;
}

/* wait for a user keypress, then clean up and exit */

getch();

retValue = gxSetMode(gxTEXT);
if(retValue < 0)
{
    PrintError("gxSetMode", retValue);
    return;
}

return;
}
```

grDrawSquare

This function draws a square at the specified coordinates.

Syntax: `int far pascal grDrawSquare(x, y, side, fillFlag)`

Parameter: x, y

Type: `int`

Description: Upper-left corner of rectangle.

Parameter: `side`

Type: `int`

Description: Size of each side in pixels.

Parameter: `fillFlag`

Type: `int`

Description: Outline and fill specifier.

Comments: The square, which has each side set to `side`, is drawn at the specified coordinates using the current line style and thickness and the current foreground color and fill style. The table in the function page for `grDrawRect` shows the five main draw/fill routines and the three routines affecting color and style for `grDrawSquare`.

Return value: Success returns `gxSUCCESS`. Failure returns an error code (negative value).

See also: `grGetLineStyle`, `grSetLineStyle`, `grGetColor`, `grSetColor`, `grGetFillStyle`, `grSetFillStyle`

Example:

```
/*--------------------------------------------------------

Filename: grDSQ.C

Function: grDrawSquare

Description: Draws a green square on the screen at 0,0

Prerequisite Function(s): gxSetDisplay
                          gxSetMode
                          grSetFillStyle
```

```
See PrintError() function described in Appendix A

-------------------------------------------------------*/

#include <stdio.h>
#include <stdlib.h>
#include <conio.h>

#include <gxlib.h>
#include <grlib.h>

void PrintError(char * funcName, int retCode);

void
main()
{
    int retValue;          /* Return value storage   */
    int dispMode;          /* 640x480x16 color       */

    /* Local initialization section */

    dispMode = gxVGA_12;   /* Set up 640x480x16 colors */
    retValue = 0;          /* Start clean              */

    /* Mandatory kernel initialization */

    retValue = gxSetDisplay(dispMode);
    if(retValue < 0)
    {
        PrintError("gxSetDisplay", retValue);
        return;
    }

    /* Let's set up our desired video mode */

    retValue = gxSetMode(gxGRAPHICS);
    if(retValue < 0)
    {
        PrintError("gxSetMode", retValue);
        return;
    }

    /*
        The fill style and color must be set
        before doing a grDrawSquare
    */
```

```
retValue = grSetFillStyle(grFSOLID, grGREEN,
            grOPAQUE);
if(retValue < 0)
{
    PrintError("grSetFillStyle", retValue);
    return;
}

/* Draw a square at screen coordinates 0,0 */

retValue = grDrawSquare(0,0, 100, grFILL);
if(retValue < 0)
{
    PrintError("grDrawSquare", retValue);
    return;
}

/* Wait for a user keypress, then clean up and exit */

getch();

retValue = gxSetMode(gxTEXT);
if(retValue < 0)
{
    PrintError("gxSetMode", retValue);
    return;
}

    return;
}
```

GRFLOODFILL

This function fills an enclosed area with the current foreground color.

Syntax: `int far pascal grFloodFill(x, y, borderColor)`

Parameter: x, y

Type: `int`

Description: Starting flood fill coordinates.

Parameter: `borderColor`

Type: `int`

Description: Color at which to stop filling.

Comments: This function fills an enclosed area of pixels with the current drawing color and style, starting at the seed point x,y and continuing until it reaches the color `borderColor`. Notice that the flood fill algorithm uses the kernel's internal buffer, which is not very large. If this function returns with the error code `gxERR_BUFSMALL`, create your own large buffer (in global memory space) and reference it in a call to the function `gxSetBuffer`, which uses your buffer and the kernel's internal buffer. Make your buffer large enough to eliminate this error code. To retrieve the current fill color and style, call `grGetColor` and `grGetFillStyle`, respectively. To change the current fill color and style, call `grSetColor` and `grSetFillStyle`, respectively.

Return value: Success returns `gxSUCCESS`. Failure returns an error code (negative value).

See also: `grSetBuffer`, `grGetLineStyle`, `grSetLineStyle`, `grGetColor`, `grSetColor`, `grGetFillStyle`, `grSetFillStyle`

Example:

```
/*- - - - - - - - - - - - - - - - - - - - - - - - - - - - - - - - - - - - - - - - - - - - - - - - - -

Filename: grFF.C

Function: grFloodFill

Description: Draws a red outline square on the screen,
            and fills it with green

Prerequisite Function(s): gxSetDisplay
                          gxSetMode
                          grSetFillStyle
                          grSetColor
                          grDrawSquare

See PrintError() function described in Appendix A

- - - - - - - - - - - - - - - - - - - - - - - - - - - - - - - - - - - - - - - - - - - - - - -*/
```

```
#include <stdio.h>
#include <stdlib.h>
#include <conio.h>

#include <gxlib.h>
#include <grlib.h>

void PrintError(char * funcName, int retCode);

void
main()
{
    int retValue;         /* Return value storage    */
    int dispMode;         /* 640x480x16 color        */

    /* Local initialization section */

    dispMode = gxVGA_12;  /* Set up 640x480x16 colors */
    retValue = 0;         /* Start clean               */

    /* Mandatory kernel initialization */

    retValue = gxSetDisplay(dispMode);
    if(retValue < 0)
    {
        PrintError("gxSetDisplay", retValue);
        return;
    }

    /* Let's set up our desired video mode */

    retValue = gxSetMode(gxGRAPHICS);
    if(retValue < 0)
    {
        PrintError("gxSetMode", retValue);
        return;
    }

    /* Set outline color to red */

    retValue = grSetColor(gxRED);
    if(retValue < 0)
```

```
{
    PrintError("grSetColor", retValue);
    return;
}

/* Set fill style and color */

retValue = grSetFillStyle(grFTHHATCH, grGREEN,
            grOPAQUE);
if(retValue < 0)
{
    PrintError("grSetFillStyle", retValue);
    return;
}

/* Draw a square at screen coordinates 50,50 */

retValue = grDrawSquare(50,50, 100, grOUTLINE);
if(retValue < 0)
{
    PrintError("grDrawSquare", retValue);
    return;
}

/* Wait for first user keypress */

getch();

retValue = grFloodFill(60,60, grRED);
if(retValue < 0)
{
    PrintError("grFloodFill", retValue);
    return;
}

/* Wait for a last user keypress, clean up and exit */

getch();

retValue = gxSetMode(gxTEXT);
if(retValue < 0)
{
    PrintError("gxSetMode", retValue);
    return;
}
```

```
      return;
}
```

GRGETACTIVEPAGE

This function returns the currently active drawing page, which may or may not be the page being displayed.

Syntax: `int far pascal grGetActivePage(void)`

Parameter: None

Comments: To find the page being viewed on the display, use `gxGetPage` in Chapter 1.

Return value: The return value is the active page number.

See also: `grSetActivePage, gxGetPage, gxSetPage`

Example:

```
/*----------------------------------------------------------

Filename: grGAP.C

Function: grGetActivePage

Description: Returns the active page

Prerequisite Function(s): gxSetDisplay

See PrintError() function described in Appendix A

----------------------------------------------------*/

#include <stdio.h>
#include <stdlib.h>
#include <conio.h>

#include <gxlib.h>
#include <grlib.h>

void PrintError(char * funcName, int retCode);

void
```

```
main()
{
    int retValue;           /* Return value storage     */
    int dispMode;           /* 640x350x16 color         */

    /* Local initialization section */

    dispMode = gxEGA_10;   /* Set up 640x350x16 colors */
    retValue = 0;          /* Start clean              */

    /* Mandatory kernel initialization */

    retValue = gxSetDisplay(dispMode);
    if(retValue < 0)
    {
        PrintError("gxSetDisplay", retValue);
        return;
    }

    retValue = grGetActivePage();

    printf("Active Page is %d\n", retValue);

    return;
}
```

GRGETBKCOLOR

This function returns the current background color.

Syntax: `int far pascal grGetBkColor(void)`

Parameter: None

Comments: The current background color is set with a call to the function grSetBkColor.

Return value: Success returns gxSUCCESS. Failure returns an error code (negative value).

See also: grSetBkColor

Example:

```
/*----------------------------------------------------

Filename: grGBC.C

Function: grGetBkColor

Description: Returns the current background color

Prerequisite Function(s): gxSetDisplay

See PrintError() function described in Appendix A

----------------------------------------------------*/

#include <stdio.h>
#include <stdlib.h>
#include <conio.h>

#include <gxlib.h>
#include <grlib.h>

void PrintError(char * funcName, int retCode);

void
main()
{
    int retValue;        /* Return value storage    */
    int dispMode;        /* 640x350x16 color        */

    /* Local initialization section */

    dispMode = gxEGA_10;  /* Set up 640x350x16 colors */
    retValue = 0;         /* Start clean               */

    /* Mandatory kernel initialization */

    retValue = gxSetDisplay(dispMode);
    if(retValue < 0)
    {
        PrintError("gxSetDisplay", retValue);
        return;
    }

    /* Get the current background color */
```

```
retValue = grGetBkColor();

printf("Background Color is %d\n", retValue);

return;
}
```

GRGETCLIPPING

This function returns the current clipping status previously set by grSetClipping. The clipping status determines whether drawing commands are clipped outside the clipping region.

Syntax: int far pascal grGetClipping(void)

Parameter: None

Comments: This function does not return the coordinates that make up the clipping region; it returns only whether there will be any clipping. To set the clipping status, see grSetClipping. To set the clipping coordinates, see grSetClipRegion. You must *first* call grSetClipRegion to establish valid clipping regions.

Return value: The return value is current clipping status (either the constant grCLIP or grNOCLIP).

See also: grSetClipping, grGetClipRegion, grSetClipRegion

Example:

```
/*-----------------------------------------------------

Filename: grGCL.C

Function: grGetClipping

Description: Sets the clipping region coordinates,
            enables clipping, and returns clipping
            status, which will be enabled

Prerequisite Function(s): gxSetDisplay
                          gxSetMode
```

```
                              grSetClipRegion
                              grSetClipping

See PrintError() function described in Appendix A

- - - - - - - - - - - - - - - - - - - - - - - - - - - - - - - - - - - - - - - - - - - - - - - - - - - - - - - - */

#include <stdio.h>
#include <stdlib.h>
#include <conio.h>

#include <gxlib.h>
#include <grlib.h>

void PrintError(char * funcName, int retCode);

void
main()
{
    int retValue;           /* Return value storage    */
    int dispMode;           /* 640x480x16 color        */

    /* Local initialization section */

    dispMode = gxVGA_12;    /* Set up 640x480x16 colors */
    retValue = 0;           /* Start clean               */

    /* Mandatory kernel initialization */

    retValue = gxSetDisplay(dispMode);
    if(retValue < 0)
    {
        PrintError("gxSetDisplay", retValue);
        return;
    }

    /* Let's set up our desired video mode */

    retValue = gxSetMode(gxGRAPHICS);
    if(retValue < 0)
    {
        PrintError("gxSetMode", retValue);
        return;
    }

    /* Set the clipping region */
```

```
retValue = grSetClipRegion(20,20, 100,100);
if(retValue < 0)
{
    PrintError("grSetClipRegion", retValue);
    return;
}

/* Enable Clipping */

retValue = grSetClipping(grCLIP);
if(retValue < 0)
{
    PrintError("grSetClipping", retValue);
    return;
}

/* Get clipping status */

retValue = grGetClipping();
if(retValue < 0)
{
    PrintError("grGetClipping", retValue);
    return;
}

/* Print the status */

printf("Clipping status is ");
if(retValue == grCLIP)
    printf("grCLIP\n");
else
    printf("grNOCLIP\n");

/* Wait for a user keypress, then clean up and exit */

getch();

retValue = gxSetMode(gxTEXT);
if(retValue < 0)
{
    PrintError("gxSetMode", retValue);
    return;
}

return;
}
```

GRGETCLIPREGION

This function returns the clipping region coordinates into the specified integer locations.

Syntax: `int far pascal grGetClipRegion(x1, y1, x2, y2)`

Parameter: x1, y1

Type: `int *`

Description: Location to store upper-left corner of clip region.

Parameter: x2, y2

Type: `int *`

Description: Location to store lower-right corner of clip region.

Comments: This function returns the region coordinates previously set with a call to `grSetClipRegion`.

Return value: Success returns `gxSUCCESS`. Failure returns an error code (negative value).

See also: `grSetClipping`, `grSetClipRegion`

Example:

```
/*-----------------------------------------------------

Filename: grGCR.C

Function: grGetClipRegion

Description: Sets the clipping region coordinates, then
            gets them. See grSetClipping for a clipping
            example

Prerequisite Function(s): gxSetDisplay
                          gxSetMode
                          grSetClipRegion

See PrintError() function described in Appendix A

-----------------------------------------------------*/
```

```c
#include <stdio.h>
#include <stdlib.h>
#include <conio.h>

#include <gxlib.h>
#include <grlib.h>

void PrintError(char * funcName, int retCode);

void
main()
{
    int retValue;        /* Return value storage      */
    int dispMode;        /* 640x480x16 color          */
    int x1,y1,x2,y2;     /* Clip region coordinates   */

    /* Local initialization section */

    dispMode = gxVGA_12;  /* Set up 640x480x16 colors */
    retValue = 0;         /* Start clean               */

    /* Mandatory kernel initialization */

    retValue = gxSetDisplay(dispMode);
    if(retValue < 0)
    {
        PrintError("gxSetDisplay", retValue);
        return;
    }

    /* Let's set up our desired video mode */

    retValue = gxSetMode(gxGRAPHICS);
    if(retValue < 0)
    {
        PrintError("gxSetMode", retValue);
        return;
    }

    /* Set the clipping region */

    retValue = grSetClipRegion(20,20, 100,100);
    if(retValue < 0)
    {
        PrintError("grSetClipRegion", retValue);
        return;
    }
```

```
/* Get the clipping region coordinates */

retValue = grGetClipRegion(&x1,&y1, &x2,&y2);
if(retValue < 0)
{
    PrintError("grGetClipRegion", retValue);
    return;
}

printf("Clip region upper left  corner is %d,%d\n",
                                        x1,y1);
printf("Clip region lower right corner is %d,%d\n",
                                        x2,y2);

/* Wait for a user keypress, then clean up and exit */

getch();

retValue = gxSetMode(gxTEXT);
if(retValue < 0)
{
    PrintError("gxSetMode", retValue);
    return;
}

return;
}
```

GRGETCOLOR

This function returns the current color used for all drawing operations.

Syntax: `int far pascal grGetColor(void)`

Parameter: None.

Comments: Use this color when plotting pixels, lines, circles, and all other drawing operations. The current drawing color is set with a call to the function `grSetColor`.

Return value: Success returns `gxSUCCESS`. Failure returns an error code (negative value).

Return value: The current drawing color.

See also: grSetColor

Example:

```
/*-------------------------------------------------------

Filename: grGC.C

Function: grGetColor

Description: Returns the current background color

Prerequisite Function(s): gxSetDisplay

See PrintError() function described in Appendix A

-----------------------------------------------------*/

#include <stdio.h>
#include <stdlib.h>
#include <conio.h>

#include <gxlib.h>
#include <grlib.h>

void PrintError(char * funcName, int retCode);

void
main()
{
    int retValue;          /* Return value storage    */
    int dispMode;          /* 640x350x16 color        */

    /* Local initialization section */

    dispMode = gxEGA_10;   /* Set up 640x350x16 colors */
    retValue = 0;          /* Start clean               */

    /* Mandatory kernel initialization */

    retValue = gxSetDisplay(dispMode);
    if(retValue < 0)
    {
        PrintError("gxSetDisplay", retValue);
        return;
    }
```

```
/* Get the current drawing color */

retValue = grGetColor( );

printf("Current Drawing Color is %d\n", retValue);

return;
}
```

grGetFillPattern

This function returns requested fill pattern into the specified 8-byte buffer.

Syntax: `int far pascal grGetFillPattern(style, pattern)`

Parameter: `style`

Type: `int`

Description: Fill style of desired pattern.

Parameter: `pattern`

Type: `char *`

Description: Location to store 8-byte pattern buffer.

Comments: Make sure the buffer is an array of at least eight bytes (for example, `char buf[8]`). The eight bits in each byte returned into the array represent one horizontal line of eight pixels. Therefore, the fill pattern will be an 8x8 pixel block. Call the function `grSetFillPattern` to change the current fill pattern to your new pattern. See Appendix A for a list of valid fill pattern styles.

Return value: Success returns `gxSUCCESS`. Failure returns an error code (negative value).

See also: `grSetClipping, grSetClipRegion`

Example:

```
/*------------------------------------------------------

Filename: grGFP.C

Function: grGetFillPattern

Description: Gets the fill pattern for FHATCH, and
            prints the hatch pattern in binary format

Prerequisite Function(s): gxSetDisplay

See PrintError() function described in Appendix A

------------------------------------------------------*/

#include <stdio.h>
#include <stdlib.h>
#include <conio.h>

#include <gxlib.h>
#include <grlib.h>

void PrintError(char * funcName, int retCode);

/* Globals variables here... */

char fillPattern[8];

void
main()
{
    int retValue;        /* Return value storage   */
    int j,cnt;           /* General purpose counters */
    int dispMode;        /* 640x480x16 color       */
    char gBuf[20];       /* General purpose buffer */

    /* Local initialization section */

    dispMode = gxVGA_12;  /* Set up 640x480x16 colors */
    retValue = 0;         /* Start clean             */

    /* Mandatory kernel initialization */
```

```
retValue = gxSetDisplay(dispMode);
if(retValue < 0)
{
    PrintError("gxSetDisplay", retValue);
    return;
}

/* Get bytes that make a grFHATCH fill pattern */

retValue = grGetFillPattern(grFHATCH, fillPattern);
if(retValue < 0)
{
    PrintError("grGetFillPattern", retValue);
    return;
}

/*
    Print two copies of the buffer side-by-side
    in binary format to aid in seeing the pattern
*/

printf("The fill pattern for grFHATCH is:\n\n");

for (j=0; j<2; j++)
{
  for(cnt=0; cnt<8; cnt++)
  {
      (void) itoa((unsigned char)fillPattern[cnt],
                  gBuf, 2);
      printf("  %08s%08s\n", gBuf, gBuf);
  }
}

return;
}
```

GRGETFILLSTYLE

This function returns the current fill pattern style, fill pattern color, and fill pattern transparency into the specified locations.

Syntax: `int far pascal grGetFillStyle(style, color, trans)`

Parameter: `style`

Type: int *

Description: Location to store fill pattern style.

Parameter: color

Type: int *

Description: Location to store fill pattern color.

Parameter: trans

Type: int *

Description: Location to store fill pattern transparency setting.

Comments: These fill pattern settings are programmed with a call to grSetFillStyle. See Appendix A for a list of the available fill pattern styles and colors. The transparency style is either the constant grTRANS or grOPAQUE.

Return value: The current fill style is not a success/failure code.

See also: grSetClipping, grSetClipRegion

Example:
```
/*- - - - - - - - - - - - - - - - - - - - - - - - - - - - - - - - - - - - - - - - - - - - - -

Filename: grGFS.C

Function: grGetFillStyle

Description: Sets new fill style and color, and then
            gets them. See the appendix for what the
            return values represent.

Prerequisite Function(s): gxSetDisplay
                          gxSetMode
                          grSetFillStyle
```

```
See PrintError() function described in Appendix A

- - - - - - - - - - - - - - - - - - - - - - - - - - - - - - - - - - - - - - - - - - - */

#include <stdio.h>
#include <stdlib.h>
#include <conio.h>

#include <gxlib.h>
#include <grlib.h>

void PrintError(char * funcName, int retCode);

void
main()
{
    int retValue;       /* Return value storage     */
    int dispMode;       /* 640x480x16 color         */
    int fStyle;         /* Fill Style storage       */
    int fColor;         /* Fill Color storage       */
    int fTrans;         /* Transparency storage     */

    /* Local initialization section */

    dispMode = gxVGA_12;  /* Set up 640x480x16 colors */
    retValue = 0;         /* Start clean              */

    /* Mandatory kernel initialization */

    retValue = gxSetDisplay(dispMode);
    if(retValue < 0)
    {
        PrintError("gxSetDisplay", retValue);
        return;
    }

    /* Let's set up our desired video mode */

    retValue = gxSetMode(gxGRAPHICS);
    if(retValue < 0)
    {
        PrintError("gxSetMode", retValue);
        return;
    }
```

```
/*
   Set the fill style, color, and
   transparency type
*/

retValue = grSetFillStyle(grFHATCH, grBLUE,
            grOPAQUE);
if(retValue < 0)
{
    PrintError("grSetFillStyle", retValue);
    return;
}

/* Get the previously defined settings */

retValue = grGetFillStyle(&fStyle, &fColor,
            &fTrans);
if(retValue < 0)
{
    PrintError("grGetFillStyle", retValue);
    return;
}

printf("Fill Style = %d\n", fStyle);
printf("Fill Color = %d\n", fColor);
printf("Fill Trans = ");

if(retValue == grTRANS)
    printf("grTRANS\n");
else
    printf("grOPAQUE\n");

/* Wait for a user keypress, then clean up and exit */

getch();

retValue = gxSetMode(gxTEXT);
if(retValue < 0)
{
    PrintError("gxSetMode", retValue);
    return;
}

return;
}
```

grGetLineStyle

This function returns the current line style and thickness.

Syntax: `int far pascal grGetLineStyle(style, thickness)`

Parameter: `style`

Type: `int *`

Description: Location to store line style.

Parameter: `thickness`

Type: `int *`

Description: Location to store line thickness.

Comments: Program these line style settings with a call to `grSetLineStyle`. Any number may be returned into the style location because the value is simply an 16-bit value representing 16 horizontal pixels. See `grSetLineStyle` for a list of predefined line styles. The thickness value returned is in pixels. Its value has no real restrictions.

Return value: Success returns `gxSUCCESS`. Failure returns an error code (negative value).

See also: `grSetLineStyle`

Example:

```
/*-------------------------------------------------------

Filename: grGLS.C

Function: grGetLineStyle

Description: Sets the line style to arbtrary values,
            then gets them, and prints them to the
            screen

Prerequisite Function(s): gxSetDisplay
                          grSetLineStyle
```

```
See PrintError() function described in Appendix A

------------------------------------------------------*/

#include <stdio.h>
#include <stdlib.h>
#include <conio.h>

#include <gxlib.h>
#include <grlib.h>

void PrintError(char * funcName, int retCode);

void
main()
{
    int retValue;          /* Return value storage    */
    int dispMode;          /* 640x480x16 color        */
    int style;             /* line style storage      */
    int thickness;         /* line thickness storage  */
    unsigned mask;         /* mask storage            */

    /* Local initialization section */

    dispMode = gxVGA_12;   /* Set up 640x480x16 colors */
    retValue = 0;          /* Start clean             */

    /* Mandatory kernel initialization */

    retValue = gxSetDisplay(dispMode);
    if(retValue < 0)
    {
        PrintError("gxSetDisplay", retValue);
        return;
    }

    /* Set the line style to arbitrary values */

    retValue = grSetLineStyle(0xF5C4, 3);
    if(retValue < 0)
    {
        PrintError("grSetLineStyle", retValue);
        return;
    }

    /* Get the preset line style & thickness */
```

```
retValue = grGetLineStyle(&style, &thickness);
if(retValue < 0)
{
    PrintError("grGetLineStyle", retValue);
    return;
}

printf("Line style is: ");
for (mask = 0x8000; mask != 0; mask >>= 1)
{
  if (style & mask)
    printf("_");
  else
    printf(" ");
}
printf(" (%X)\n", style);

printf("\nLine thickness = %d\n", thickness);

return;
}
```

GRGETMOUSEBUTTONS

This function returns the current mouse button flags.

Syntax: `int far pascal grGetMouseButtons(void)`

Parameter: None.

Comments: Depending on its state, the value returned has a unique bit set or is cleared for each button. Use the following mouse button constants as bitwise masks to find the state of each button.

Button: `grLBUTTON`

Description: Left button bit mask.

Button: `grMBUTTON`

Description: Middle button bit mask.

Button: grRBUTTON

Description: Right button bit mask.

Return value: The state of mouse buttons.

See also: grGetMousePresses, grGetMouseReleases

Example:

```
/*----------------------------------------------------------

Filename: grGMB.C

Function: grGetMouseButtons

Description: Displays the mouse; then turns it off after
             a keypress

Prerequisite Function(s): gxSetDisplay
                          gxSetMode
                          grInitMouse
                          grTrackMouse
                          grDisplayMouse
                          grStopMouse

See PrintError() function described in Appendix A

----------------------------------------------------------*/

#include <stdio.h>
#include <stdlib.h>
#include <conio.h>

#include <gxlib.h>
#include <grlib.h>

void PrintError(char * funcName, int retCode);

void
main()
{
    int retValue;      /* Return value storage    */
    int dispMode;      /* 640x480x16 color        */
```

```
/* Local initialization section */

dispMode = gxVGA_12;   /* Set up 640x480x16 colors */
retValue = 0;          /* Start clean              */

/* Mandatory kernel initialization */

retValue = gxSetDisplay(dispMode);
if(retValue < 0)
{
    PrintError("gxSetDisplay", retValue);
    return;
}

/* Let's set up our desired video mode */

retValue = gxSetMode(gxGRAPHICS);
if(retValue < 0)
{
    PrintError("gxSetMode", retValue);
    return;
}

/* Initialize and install mouse driver */

retValue = grInitMouse();
if(retValue < 0)
{
    PrintError("grInitMouse", retValue);
    return;
}

/* Track the mouse movement */

retValue = grTrackMouse(grTRACK);
if(retValue < 0)
{
    PrintError("grTrackMouse", retValue);
    return;
}

/* Turn the mouse on */

retValue = grDisplayMouse(grSHOW);
if(retValue < 0)
```

```
{
    PrintError("grDisplayMouse", retValue);
    return;
}

/* Loop, waiting for a mouse button press */

while(!(retValue = grGetMouseButtons()));

/* Print the button settings */

printf("The left   mouse button was ");
if((retValue&grLBUTTON) != grLBUTTON)
    printf("not ");
printf("pressed\n");

printf("The middle mouse button was ");
if((retValue&grMBUTTON) != grMBUTTON)
    printf("not ");
printf("pressed\n");

printf("The right  mouse button was ");
if((retValue&grRBUTTON) != grRBUTTON)
    printf("not ");
printf("pressed\n");

/* Wait for a user keypress */

getch();

/* Turn the mouse off */

retValue = grDisplayMouse(grHIDE);
if(retValue < 0)
{
    PrintError("grDisplayMouse", retValue);
    return;
}

/* De-init and remove mouse driver */

retValue = grStopMouse();
if(retValue < 0)
```

```
    {
        PrintError("grStopMouse", retValue);
        return;
    }

    /* Return to text mode */

    retValue = gxSetMode(gxTEXT);
    if(retValue < 0)
    {
        PrintError("gxSetMode", retValue);
        return;
    }

    return;
}
```

grGetMouseMask

This function returns the mouse cursor and mask for a given mouse style.

Syntax: `int far pascal grGetMouseMask(style, hotx, hoty, cursor, mask)`

Parameter: `style`

Type: `int`

Description: Mouse style from which to retrieve masks.

Parameter: `hotx, hoty`

Type: `int *`

Description: Storage locations for mouse cursor hotspot.

Parameter: `cursor`

Type: `int *`

Description: Storage location for mouse cursor array.

Parameter: mask

Type: int *

Description: Storage location for mouse mask array.

Comments: For a given mouse style, this function returns the current mouse cursor masks into the 16-word buffers pointed to by cursor and mask. Each word in the pattern corresponds to 16 pixels. Whenever a bit in a mask byte is 1, the pixel will be plotted. The hotspot coordinates returned represent the cursor's hotspot location (the tip of the arrow, middle of the crosshair, and so on).

Return value: Success returns gxSUCCESS. Failure returns an error code (negative value).

See also: grSetMousePos

Example:

```
/*-------------------------------------------------------

Filename: grGMM.C

Function: grGetMouseMask

Description: Gets the mouse mask for mouse grCARROW, and
            prints the mask in binary format

Prerequisite Function(s): gxSetDisplay

See PrintError() function described in Appendix A

-----------------------------------------------------*/

#include <stdio.h>
#include <stdlib.h>
#include <conio.h>

#include <gxlib.h>
#include <grlib.h>

void PrintError(char * funcName, int retCode);

/* Globals variables here... */
```

```
int  ax,ay;
int  acurs[16],amask[16];

void
main()
{
    int retValue;        /* Return value storage    */
    int cnt;             /* General purpose counters */
    int dispMode;        /* 640x480x16 color        */
    char gBuf[20];       /* General purpose buffer  */

    /* Local initialization section */

    dispMode = gxVGA_12;  /* Set up 640x480x16 colors */
    retValue = 0;         /* Start clean              */

    /* Mandatory kernel initialization */

    retValue = gxSetDisplay(dispMode);
    if(retValue < 0)
    {
        PrintError("gxSetDisplay", retValue);
        return;
    }

    /* Get bytes that make a grCARROW mouse cursor */

    retValue = grGetMouseMask(grCARROW, &ax, &ay,
                              acurs, amask);
    if(retValue < 0)
    {
        PrintError("grGetMouseMask", retValue);
        return;
    }

    /*
       Print the cursor and the mask in binary format
    */

    printf("The cursor for grCARROW is:    ");
    printf("The mask    for grCARROW is:\n\n");

    for(cnt=0; cnt<16; cnt++)
    {
        (void) itoa((unsigned int)acurs[cnt], gBuf, 2);
        printf("    %016s          ", gBuf, gBuf);
```

```
      (void) itoa((unsigned int)amask[cnt], gBuf, 2);
      printf("    %016s\n", gBuf, gBuf);
   }
   printf("\n\n");

   return;
}
```

grGetMousePos

This function returns the current mouse position.

Syntax: `int far pascal grGetMousePos(x, y)`

Parameter: x, y

Type: `int *`

Description: Storage locations for mouse position.

Comments: The coordinates returned always represent screen coordinates and are representative of the cursor's hotspot location (the tip of the arrow, middle of the crosshair, and so on). The mouse cursor moves even when it is hidden, and you can track its coordinates.

Return value: Success returns `gxSUCCESS`. Failure returns an error code (negative value).

See also: `grSetMousePos`

Example:

```
/*-----------------------------------------------------

Filename: grGMP.C

Function: grGetMousePos

Description: Displays the mouse, waits for a keypress,
            and returns the mouse position

Prerequisite Function(s): gxSetDisplay
                          gxSetMode
                          grInitMouse
                          grTrackMouse
```

```
                              grStopMouse
                              grDisplayMouse

See PrintError() function described in Appendix A

-------------------------------------------------------*/

#include <stdio.h>
#include <stdlib.h>
#include <conio.h>

#include <gxlib.h>
#include <grlib.h>

void PrintError(char * funcName, int retCode);

void
main()
{
    int retValue;        /* Return value storage    */
    int dispMode;        /* 640x480x16 color        */
    int x, y;            /* Mouse Pos storage       */

    /* Local initialization section */

    dispMode = gxVGA_12;  /* Set up 640x480x16 colors */
    retValue = 0;         /* Start clean              */

    /* Mandatory kernel initialization */

    retValue = gxSetDisplay(dispMode);
    if(retValue < 0)
    {
        PrintError("gxSetDisplay", retValue);
        return;
    }

    /* Let's set up our desired video mode */

    retValue = gxSetMode(gxGRAPHICS);
    if(retValue < 0)
    {
        PrintError("gxSetMode", retValue);
        return;
    }
```

```
/* Initialize and install mouse driver */

retValue = grInitMouse();
if(retValue < 0)
{
    PrintError("grInitMouse", retValue);
    return;
}

/* Track the mouse movement */

retValue = grTrackMouse(grTRACK);
if(retValue < 0)
{
    PrintError("grTrackMouse", retValue);
    return;
}

/* Turn the mouse on */

retValue = grDisplayMouse(grSHOW);
if(retValue < 0)
{
    PrintError("grDisplayMouse", retValue);
    return;
}

/* Wait for a user keypress */

getch();

retValue = grGetMousePos(&x, &y);
if(retValue < 0)
{
    PrintError("grGetMousePos", retValue);
    return;
}

/* Print mouse position, get a key */

printf("Mouse Position is %d,%d; ", x,y);
printf("Hit any key to exit... ");
getch();

/* Turn the mouse off */

retValue = grDisplayMouse(grHIDE);
```

```
    if(retValue < 0)
    {
        PrintError("grDisplayMouse", retValue);
        return;
    }

    /* De-init and remove mouse driver */

    retValue = grStopMouse();
    if(retValue < 0)
    {
        PrintError("grStopMouse", retValue);
        return;
    }

    /* Return to text mode */

    retValue = gxSetMode(gxTEXT);
    if(retValue < 0)
    {
        PrintError("gxSetMode", retValue);
        return;
    }

    return;
}
```

GRGETMOUSEPRESSES

This function returns the number of mouse button presses since the last request.

Syntax: `int far pascal grGetMousePresses(button, presses, x, y)`

Parameter: `button`

Type: `int`

Description: Mouse button to check.

Parameter: presses

Type: int *

Description: Storage locations for mouse press count.

Parameter: x, y

Type: int *

Description: Storage locations for mouse position.

Comments: This function is similar to grGetMouseReleases, except it returns button press information. See the function grGetMouseButtons for a list of valid mouse button identifiers. The number of mouse presses since the last call is placed at the location pointed to by presses. The coordinates where the mouse was at the last button press are stored in x,y. You can use this function to wait for mouse input, without polling the mouse with a grGetMouseButtons loop.

Return value: Success returns gxSUCCESS. Failure returns an error code (negative value).

See also: grGetMouseButtons, grGetMouseReleases

Example:

```
/*----------------------------------------------------

Filename: grGMPR.C

Function: grGetMousePresses

Description: Displays the mouse, waits for a keypress,
            and returns number of mouse presses before
            the keypress

Prerequisite Function(s): gxSetDisplay
                          gxSetMode
                          grInitMouse
                          grTrackMouse
                          grStopMouse
                          grDisplayMouse
```

```
See PrintError() function described in Appendix A

------------------------------------------------------*/

#include <stdio.h>
#include <stdlib.h>
#include <conio.h>

#include <gxlib.h>
#include <grlib.h>

void PrintError(char * funcName, int retCode);

void
main()
{
    int retValue;          /* Return value storage      */
    int dispMode;          /* 640x480x16 color          */
    int x, y;              /* Mouse Pos storage         */
    int presses;           /* Mouse presses storage     */

    /* Local initialization section */

    dispMode = gxVGA_12;   /* Set up 640x480x16 colors */
    retValue = 0;          /* Start clean              */

    /* Mandatory kernel initialization */

    retValue = gxSetDisplay(dispMode);
    if(retValue < 0)
    {
        PrintError("gxSetDisplay", retValue);
        return;
    }

    /* Let's set up our desired video mode */

    retValue = gxSetMode(gxGRAPHICS);
    if(retValue < 0)
    {
        PrintError("gxSetMode", retValue);
        return;
    }

    /* Initialize and install mouse driver */
```

```
retValue = grInitMouse();
if(retValue < 0)
{
    PrintError("grInitMouse", retValue);
    return;
}

/* Track the mouse movement */

retValue = grTrackMouse(grTRACK);
if(retValue < 0)
{
    PrintError("grTrackMouse", retValue);
    return;
}

/* Turn the mouse on */

retValue = grDisplayMouse(grSHOW);
if(retValue < 0)
{
    PrintError("grDisplayMouse", retValue);
    return;
}

/* Wait for a user keypress */

getch();

/* Get the number of mouse presses */

retValue = grGetMousePresses(grLBUTTON, &presses,
                            &x, &y);
if(retValue < 0)
{
    PrintError("grGetMousePresses", retValue);
    return;
}

/* Print mouse position, get a key */

printf("There were %d presses. ", presses);
printf("The last press was at %d,%d\n\n", x,y);
printf("Hit any key to exit... ");
getch();
```

```
/* Turn the mouse off */

retValue = grDisplayMouse(grHIDE);
if(retValue < 0)
{
    PrintError("grDisplayMouse", retValue);
    return;
}

/* De-init and remove mouse driver */

retValue = grStopMouse();
if(retValue < 0)
{
    PrintError("grStopMouse", retValue);
    return;
}

/* Return to text mode */

retValue = gxSetMode(gxTEXT);
if(retValue < 0)
{
    PrintError("gxSetMode", retValue);
    return;
}

    return;
}
```

GRGETMOUSERELEASES

This function returns the number of mouse button releases since the last request.

Syntax: int far pascal grGetMouseReleases(button, releases, x, y)

Parameter: button

Type: int

Description: Mouse button to check.

Parameter: `releases`

Type: `int *`

Description: Storage locations for mouse release count.

Parameter: `x, y`

Type: `int *`

Description: Storage locations for mouse position.

Comments: This function is similar to `grGetMousePresses`, except it returns button release information. See the function `grGetMouseButtons` for a list of valid mouse button identifiers. The number of mouse releases since the last call is placed at the location pointed to by `releases`. The coordinates where the mouse was at the last button release are stored in x,y. You can use this function to wait for mouse input, without polling the mouse with a `grGetMouseButtons` loop.

Return value: Success returns `gxSUCCESS`. Failure returns an error code (negative value).

See also: `grGetMouseButtons, grGetMousePresses`

Example:
```
/*- - - - - - - - - - - - - - - - - - - - - - - - - - - - - - - - - - - - - - - - - - - - - - - - - - - - - -

Filename: grGMR.C

Function: grGetMouseReleases

Description: Displays the mouse, waits for a keypress,
            and returns number of mouse releases before
            the keypress

Prerequisite Function(s): gxSetDisplay
                          gxSetMode
                          grInitMouse
```

```
                        grTrackMouse
                        grStopMouse
                        grDisplayMouse

    See PrintError() function described in Appendix A

    --------------------------------------------------------*/

    #include <stdio.h>
    #include <stdlib.h>
    #include <conio.h>

    #include <gxlib.h>
    #include <grlib.h>

    void PrintError(char * funcName, int retCode);

    void
    main()
    {
        int retValue;        /* Return value storage      */
        int dispMode;        /* 640x480x16 color          */
        int x, y;            /* Mouse Pos storage         */
        int releases;        /* Mouse releases storage    */

        /* Local initialization section */

        dispMode = gxVGA_12;  /* Set up 640x480x16 colors */
        retValue = 0;         /* Start clean              */

        /* Mandatory kernel initialization */

        retValue = gxSetDisplay(dispMode);
        if(retValue < 0)
        {
            PrintError("gxSetDisplay", retValue);
            return;
        }

        /* Let's set up our desired video mode */

        retValue = gxSetMode(gxGRAPHICS);
        if(retValue < 0)
        {
            PrintError("gxSetMode", retValue);
            return;
        }
```

```
/* Initialize and install mouse driver */

retValue = grInitMouse();
if(retValue < 0)
{
    PrintError("grInitMouse", retValue);
    return;
}

/* Track the mouse movement */

retValue = grTrackMouse(grTRACK);
if(retValue < 0)
{
    PrintError("grTrackMouse", retValue);
    return;
}

/* Turn the mouse on */

retValue = grDisplayMouse(grSHOW);
if(retValue < 0)
{
    PrintError("grDisplayMouse", retValue);
    return;
}

/* Wait for a user keypress */

getch();

/* Get the number of mouse releases */

retValue = grGetMouseReleases(grLBUTTON, &releases,
                              &x, &y);
if(retValue < 0)
{
    PrintError("grGetMouseReleases", retValue);
    return;
}

/* Print mouse position, get a key */

printf("There were %d releases. ", releases);
```

```
printf("The last release was at %d,%d\n\n", x,y);
printf("Hit any key to exit... ");
getch();

/* Turn the mouse off */

retValue = grDisplayMouse(grHIDE);
if(retValue < 0)
{
    PrintError("grDisplayMouse", retValue);
    return;
}

/* De-init and remove mouse driver */

retValue = grStopMouse();
if(retValue < 0)
{
    PrintError("grStopMouse", retValue);
    return;
}

/* Return to text mode */

retValue = gxSetMode(gxTEXT);
if(retValue < 0)
{
    PrintError("gxSetMode", retValue);
    return;
}

    return;
}
```

GRGETMOUSESTYLE

This function returns the current mouse style and color.

Syntax: `int far pascal grGetMouseStyle(style, color)`

Parameter: `style`

Type: `int *`

Description: Storage location for mouse style.

Parameter: `color`

Type: `int *`

Description: Storage location for mouse color.

Comments: The cursor's style defines its shape. You can change the mouse style and color by calling the function `grSetMouseStyle`. See `grSetMouseStyle` for a list of valid mouse styles and colors.

Return value: Success returns `gxSUCCESS`. Failure returns an error code (negative value).

See also: `grSetMouseStyle`

Example:

```
/*----------------------------------------------------

Filename: grGMS.C

Function: grGetMouseStyle

Description: Sets the current mouse style to an hour-
            glass, and the color to red, then gets it

Prerequisite Function(s): gxSetDisplay
                          grSetMouseStyle

See PrintError() function described in Appendix A

----------------------------------------------------*/

#include <stdio.h>
#include <stdlib.h>
#include <conio.h>

#include <gxlib.h>
#include <grlib.h>

void PrintError(char * funcName, int retCode);

void
```

```
main()
{
    int retValue;       /* Return value storage    */
    int dispMode;       /* 640x480x16 color        */
    int mStyle;         /* Mouse Style storage     */
    int mColor;         /* Mouse Color Storage     */

    /* Local initialization section */

    dispMode = gxVGA_12;    /* Set up 640x480x16 colors */
    retValue = 0;           /* Start clean              */

    /* Mandatory kernel initialization */

    retValue = gxSetDisplay(dispMode);
    if(retValue < 0)
    {
        PrintError("gxSetDisplay", retValue);
        return;
    }

    /*
       Set the mouse style to an hourglass,
       and the color to red.
    */

    retValue = grSetMouseStyle(grCTIME, grRED);
    if(retValue < 0)
    {
        PrintError("grSetMouseStyle", retValue);
        return;
    }

    /* Now get the new mouse style and color */

    retValue = grGetMouseStyle(&mStyle, &mColor);
    if(retValue < 0)
    {
        PrintError("grGetMouseStyle", retValue);
        return;
    }

    printf("Mouse Style = %d\n", mStyle);
    printf("Mouse Color = %d\n", mColor);

    return;
}
```

GRGETOP

This function returns the current logical operation, which is used by all drawing and text functions.

Syntax: `int far pascal grGetOp(void)`

Parameter: None.

Comments: The return value may be one of the constants `gxSET`, `gxAND`, `gxOR`, `gxXOR`. Note that these are kernel constants. Your logical operation is set with a call to `grSetOp`. See `grSetOp` for a description of each logical operation.

Return value: Return value is one of the constants `gxSET`, `gxAND`, `gxOR`, `gxXOR`.

See also: `grSetOp`, `gxPutImage`

Example:

```
/*------------------------------------------------------------

Filename: grGO.C

Function: grGetOp

Description: Sets the logical operation to gxAND, and
            then gets it

Prerequisite Function(s): gxSetDisplay
                          grSetOp

See PrintError() function described in Appendix A

-----------------------------------------------------------*/

#include <stdio.h>
#include <stdlib.h>
#include <conio.h>

#include <gxlib.h>
#include <grlib.h>

void PrintError(char * funcName, int retCode);
```

```
void
main()
{
    int retValue;        /* Return value storage   */
    int dispMode;        /* 640x480x16 color       */

    /* Local initialization section */

    dispMode = gxVGA_12;  /* Set up 640x480x16 colors */
    retValue = 0;         /* Start clean               */

    /* Mandatory kernel initialization */

    retValue = gxSetDisplay(dispMode);
    if(retValue < 0)
    {
        PrintError("gxSetDisplay", retValue);
        return;
    }

    /* Set the logical operation to AND */

    retValue = grSetOp(gxAND);
    if(retValue < 0)
    {
        PrintError("grSetOp", retValue);
        return;
    }

    /* Now get the new logical operation */

    retValue = grGetOp();
    if(retValue < 0)
    {
        PrintError("grGetOp", retValue);
        return;
    }

    printf("Logical operation is %d\n", retValue);

    return;
}
```

GrGetPixel

This function returns the pixel color value of the pixel located at the specified coordinates.

Syntax: `int far pascal grGetPixel(x, y)`

Paramter: x, y

Type: `int`

Description: Pixel coordinates.

Comments: This function returns the palette entry number for the specified pixel. To retrieve the actual Red, Green, and Blue color component values, use the returned value as the argument for the functions `gxGetPaletteColor` (EGA color modes) or `gxGetPaletteRGB` (VGA color modes).

Return value: Return value is the requested pixel color value.

See also: `gxGetPaletteColor`, `gxGetPaletteRGB`, `grPutPixel`

Example:

```
/*---------------------------------------------------

Filename: grGP.C

Function: grGetPixel

Description: Draws a blue rectangle on the screen, and
            gets the color of a pixel inside the
            rectangle

Prerequisite Function(s): gxSetDisplay
                          gxSetMode
                          grSetFillStyle
                          grDrawRect

See PrintError() function described in Appendix A

---------------------------------------------------*/
```

```c
#include <stdio.h>
#include <stdlib.h>
#include <conio.h>

#include <gxlib.h>
#include <grlib.h>

void PrintError(char * funcName, int retCode);

void
main()
{
    int retValue;          /* Return value storage    */
    int dispMode;          /* 640x480x16 color        */

    /* Local initialization section */

    dispMode = gxVGA_12;   /* Set up 640x480x16 colors */
    retValue = 0;          /* Start clean              */

    /* Mandatory kernel initialization */

    retValue = gxSetDisplay(dispMode);
    if(retValue < 0)
    {
        PrintError("gxSetDisplay", retValue);
        return;
    }

    /* Let's set up our desired video mode */

    retValue = gxSetMode(gxGRAPHICS);
    if(retValue < 0)
    {
        PrintError("gxSetMode", retValue);
        return;
    }

    /*
        The fill style and color must be set
        before doing a grDrawRect
    */

    retValue = grSetFillStyle(grFSOLID, grBLUE,
            grOPAQUE);
    if(retValue < 0)
```

```
{
    PrintError("grSetFillStyle", retValue);
    return;
}

/* Draw a rectangle */

retValue = grDrawRect(50,50, 75,100, grFILL);
if(retValue < 0)
{
    PrintError("grDrawRect", retValue);
    return;
}

/* Get a pixel value inside the rectangle */

retValue = grGetPixel(70,90);
if(retValue < 0)
{
    PrintError("grGetPixel", retValue);
    return;
}

printf("The pixel color is %d\n", retValue);

/* Wait for a user keypress, then clean up and exit */

getch();

retValue = gxSetMode(gxTEXT);
if(retValue < 0)
{
    PrintError("gxSetMode", retValue);
    return;
}

return;
}
```

GrGetState

This function returns the state of all graphics functions.

Syntax: `int far pascal grGetState(state)`

Parameter: `state`

Type: GRSTATE *

Description: Location to store graphics state information.

Comments: Use this function to save the entire state of the graphics functions and restore it at a later time with a single function call to grSetState. See Appendix A for a list of the GRSTATE structure.

Return value: Success returns gxSUCCESS. Failure returns an error code (negative value).

See also: grSetState

Example:

```
/*-----------------------------------------------------------

Filename: grGS.C

Function: grGetState

Description: Gets the current graphics state

Prerequisite Function(s): gxSetDisplay

See PrintError() function described in Appendix A

-----------------------------------------------------------*/

#include <stdio.h>
#include <stdlib.h>
#include <conio.h>

#include <gxlib.h>
#include <grlib.h>

void PrintError(char * funcName, int retCode);

/* Global variables here... */

GRSTATE graphicsState;

void
```

```
main()
{
    int retValue;        /* Return value storage   */
    int dispMode;        /* 640x350x16 color       */

    /* Local initialization section */

    dispMode = gxEGA_10;  /* Set up 640x350x16 colors */
    retValue = 0;         /* Start clean              */

    /* Mandatory kernel initialization */

    retValue = gxSetDisplay(dispMode);
    if(retValue < 0)
    {
        PrintError("gxSetDisplay", retValue);
        return;
    }

    /* Get the current graphics state */

    retValue = grGetState(&graphicsState);

    /* Print the foreground and background colors */

    printf("Current Drawing    Color is %d\n",
                    graphicsState.color);
    printf("Current Background Color is %d\n",
                    graphicsState.bkcolor);

    return;
}
```

GRGETTEXTJUSTIFY

This function returns the current text justification setting.

Syntax: `int far pascal grGetTextJustify(hJust, vJust)`

Parameter: `hJust`

Type: `int *`

Description: Storage location of horizontal justification setting.

Parameter: vJust

Type: int *

Description: Storage location of vertical justification setting.

Comments: The justification controls the placement of text displayed with grOutText. See the function grSetTextJustify for a list of valid justification codes.

Return value: Success returns gxSUCCESS. Failure returns an error code (negative value).

See also: grSetTextJustify, grOutText

Example:

```
/*--------------------------------------------------------

Filename: grGTJ.C

Function: grGetTextJustify

Description: Sets text justify to center/center, gets
            the justification values, and prints them
            on the screen right justified.

Prerequisite Function(s): gxSetDisplay
                          gxSetMode
                          grOutText
                          grMoveTo
                          grSetTextJustify

See PrintError() function described in Appendix A

-----------------------------------------------------*/

#include <stdio.h>
#include <stdlib.h>
#include <conio.h>

#include <gxlib.h>
#include <grlib.h>
```

```c
void PrintError(char * funcName, int retCode);

/* Global variables here... */

char tmpstr[256];

void
main()
{
    int retValue;          /* Return value storage    */
    int dispMode;          /* 640x480x16 color        */
    int hJust;             /* Horizontal Justify      */
    int vJust;             /* Vertical Justify        */

    /* Local initialization section */

    dispMode = gxVGA_12;   /* Set up 640x480x16 colors */
    retValue = 0;          /* Start clean              */

    /* Mandatory kernel initialization */

    retValue = gxSetDisplay(dispMode);
    if(retValue < 0)
    {
        PrintError("gxSetDisplay", retValue);
        return;
    }

    /* Let's set up our desired video mode */

    retValue = gxSetMode(gxGRAPHICS);
    if(retValue < 0)
    {
        PrintError("gxSetMode", retValue);
        return;
    }

    /* Set justification to right/top */

    retValue = grSetTextJustify(grTRIGHT, grTTOP);
    if(retValue < 0)
    {
        PrintError("grSetTextJustify", retValue);
        return;
    }
```

```
/* Place cursor pointer to end of top row */

retValue = grMoveTo(639, 0);
if(retValue < 0)
{
    PrintError("grMoveTo", retValue);
    return;
}

/* Get the justification values */

retValue = grGetTextJustify(&hJust, &vJust);
if(retValue < 0)
{
    PrintError("grGetTextJustify", retValue);
    return;
}

/*
    Print the justification return values.
    The line will be right-justified at the
    edge of the screen, and in the default
    color blue.
*/

sprintf(tmpstr,
    "HJust is %d, VJust is %d", hJust, vJust);
retValue = grOutText(tmpstr);
if(retValue < 0)
{
    PrintError("grOutText", retValue);
    return;
}

/* Get a user keypress */

getch();

/* Clean up and exit */

retValue = gxSetMode(gxTEXT);
if(retValue < 0)
{
    PrintError("gxSetMode", retValue);
```

```
      return;
   }

   return;
}
```

grGetTextStyle

This function returns the current text ROM font style and transparency setting.

Syntax: `int far pascal grGetTextStyle(style, trans)`

Parameter: `style`

Type: `int *`

Description: Location to store text style.

Parameter: `trans`

Type: `int *`

Description: Location to store text transparency setting.

Comments: Use the font style returned for all text output using `grOutText`. See the function `grSetTextStyle` for a list of valid text styles and transparency settings.

Return value: Success returns `gxSUCCESS`. Failure returns an error code (negative value).

See also: `grSetTextStyle`, `grOutText`

Example:

```
/*-----------------------------------------------------

Filename: grGTS.C

Function: grGetTextStyle

Description: Sets the text style to an 8x8 font, gets
            the font, and prints its return value
```

```
Prerequisite Function(s): gxSetDisplay
                          gxSetMode
                          grOutText
                          grSetTextStyle

See PrintError() function described in Appendix A

-------------------------------------------------------*/

#include <stdio.h>
#include <stdlib.h>
#include <conio.h>

#include <gxlib.h>
#include <grlib.h>

void PrintError(char * funcName, int retCode);

/* Global variables here... */

char tmpstr[256];

void
main()
{
    int retValue;       /* Return value storage    */
    int dispMode;       /* 640x480x16 color        */
    int style;          /* Style storage           */
    int trans;          /* Transparency storage     */

    /* Local initialization section */

    dispMode = gxVGA_12;  /* Set up 640x480x16 colors */
    retValue = 0;         /* Start clean               */

    /* Mandatory kernel initialization */

    retValue = gxSetDisplay(dispMode);
    if(retValue < 0)
    {
        PrintError("gxSetDisplay", retValue);
        return;
    }

    /* Let's set up our desired video mode */
```

```
retValue = gxSetMode(gxGRAPHICS);
if(retValue < 0)
{
    PrintError("gxSetMode", retValue);
    return;
}

/* Set the font to be 8x8, transparent */

retValue = grSetTextStyle(grTXT8X8, grTRANS);
if(retValue < 0)
{
    PrintError("grSetTextStyle", retValue);
    return;
}

retValue = grGetTextStyle(&style, &trans);
if(retValue < 0)
{
    PrintError("grGetTextStyle", retValue);
    return;
}

/*
   Print the return values.  This line will
   be at 0,0, and in the default color blue
*/

sprintf(tmpstr, "Style is %d, and trans is %d",
                                style, trans);
retValue = grOutText(tmpstr);
if(retValue < 0)
{
    PrintError("grOutText", retValue);
    return;
}

/* Get a user keypress */

getch();

/* Clean up and exit */
```

```
    retValue = gxSetMode(gxTEXT);
    if(retValue < 0)
    {
        PrintError("gxSetMode", retValue);
        return;
    }

    return;
}
```

GR**G**ET**V**IEW**P**ORT

This function returns the upper-left and lower-right coordinates of the current viewport. The viewport relocates drawing to a particular region of the screen.

Syntax: `int far pascal grGetViewPort(x1, y1, x2, y2)`

Parameter: x1, y1

Type: `int *`

Description: Location to store upper-left corner coordinates of viewport.

Parameter: x2, y2

Type: `int *`

Description: Location to store lower-right corner coordinates of viewport.

Comments: The viewport can act as a window, allowing drawing functions to take place with respect to the viewport's coordinates, without concern for the exact screen coordinates. The viewport coordinates are programmed with a call to `grSetViewPort`.

Return value: Success returns `gxSUCCESS`. Failure returns an error code (negative value).

See also: `grSetViewPort`

Example:

```
/*-----------------------------------------------------

Filename: grGVP.C

Function: grGetViewPort

Description: Sets the current viewport coordinates
             to the lower-right quadrant of the screen,
             gets the viewport coordinates, and prints
             them on the screen

Prerequisite Function(s): gxSetDisplay
                          gxSetMode
                          grSetViewPort

See PrintError() function described in Appendix A

------------------------------------------------------*/
#include <stdio.h>
#include <stdlib.h>
#include <conio.h>

#include <gxlib.h>
#include <grlib.h>

void PrintError(char * funcName, int retCode);

void
main()
{
    int retValue;          /* Return value storage   */
    int dispMode;          /* 640x480x16 color       */
    int dispColor;         /* Display Color          */
    int dispPage;          /* Display Page           */
    int x1, y1;            /* Upper-left corner      */
    int x2, y2;            /* Lower-right corner     */

    /* Local initialization section */

    dispMode = gxVGA_12;   /* Set up 640x480x16 colors */
    dispColor = gxRED;     /* Do a full red screen     */
    dispPage = 0;          /* Page 0                   */
    retValue = 0;          /* Start clean              */
```

```
/* Mandatory kernel initialization */

retValue = gxSetDisplay(dispMode);
if(retValue < 0)
{
    PrintError("gxSetDisplay", retValue);
    return;
}

/* Let's set up our desired video mode */

retValue = gxSetMode(gxGRAPHICS);
if(retValue < 0)
{
    PrintError("gxSetMode", retValue);
    return;
}

/*
    Set the viewport coordinates to be at
    the lower-right quadrant of screen
*/

retValue = grSetViewPort(320,240, 639,479);
if(retValue < 0)
{
    PrintError("grSetViewPort", retValue);
    return;
}

/* Get the current viewport coordinates */

retValue = grGetViewPort(&x1,&y1, &x2,&y2);
if(retValue < 0)
{
    PrintError("grGetViewPort", retValue);
    return;
}

printf("Upper-left  corner is %d,%d\n", x1, y1);
printf("Lower-right corner is %d,%d",   x2, y2);

/* Wait for a user keypress, then clean up and exit */

getch();
```

```
retValue = gxSetMode(gxTEXT);
if(retValue < 0)
{
    PrintError("gxSetMode", retValue);
    return;
}

    return;
}
```

GRINITMOUSE

This function initializes the mouse driver.

Syntax: `int far pascal grInitMouse(void)`

Parameter: None.

Comments: This function first determines whether there is a mouse driver, and then, if found, initializes it. If the mouse cursor currently is visible, it is hidden. Note that you *must* call this function *before* any other mouse function and that you *must* call grStopMouse *before* exiting your program, or your system may crash.

Return value: Success returns gxSUCCESS. Failure returns an error code (negative value).

See also: grDisplayMouse, grTrackMouse, grStopMouse

Example:

```
/*----------------------------------------------------

Filename: grIM.C

Function: grInitMouse

Description: Finds and initializes the mouse driver.
            This function does little else. See
            grDisplayMouse to see more stuff.

Prerequisite Function(s): gxSetDisplay
                          gxSetMode
                          grStopMouse
```

See PrintError() function described in Appendix A

```
------------------------------------------------------*/

#include <stdio.h>
#include <stdlib.h>
#include <conio.h>

#include <gxlib.h>
#include <grlib.h>

void PrintError(char * funcName, int retCode);

void
main()
{
    int retValue;          /* Return value storage    */
    int dispMode;          /* 640x480x16 color        */

    /* Local initialization section */

    dispMode = gxVGA_12;   /* Set up 640x480x16 colors */
    retValue = 0;          /* Start clean              */

    /* Mandatory kernel initialization */

    retValue = gxSetDisplay(dispMode);
    if(retValue < 0)
    {
        PrintError("gxSetDisplay", retValue);
        return;
    }

    /* Let's set up our desired video mode */

    retValue = gxSetMode(gxGRAPHICS);
    if(retValue < 0)
    {
        PrintError("gxSetMode", retValue);
        return;
    }

    /* Initialize and install mouse driver */
```

```
retValue = grInitMouse();
if(retValue < 0)
{
    PrintError("grInitMouse", retValue);
    return;
}

printf("Mouse initialized, but not displayed.\n");

/* Wait for a user keypress */

getch();

/* De-init and remove mouse driver */

retValue = grStopMouse();
if(retValue < 0)
{
    PrintError("grStopMouse", retValue);
    return;
}

/* Return to text mode */

retValue = gxSetMode(gxTEXT);
if(retValue < 0)
{
    PrintError("gxSetMode", retValue);
    return;
}

return;
}
```

GRLINEREL

This function draws a line relative to the current cursor position (CP).

Syntax: int far pascal grLineRel(dx, dy)

Parameter: dx, dy

Type: int

Description: Relative end-of-line coordinates.

Comments: If the CP is located at *x,y*, the line is drawn starting at *x,y* and ending at (*x*+dx),(*y*+dy); next, the CP is advanced to the end-of-line coordinates.

Return value: Success returns gxSUCCESS. Failure returns an error code (negative value).

See also: grLineTo, grMoveTo, grMoveRel, grOutText

Example:

```
/*------------------------------------------------------------

Filename: grLR.C

Function: grLineRel

Description: Draws a yellow line relative to the current
             cursor position, which was set to 0, 100.
             Compare with grLineTo

Prerequisite Function(s): gxSetDisplay
                          gxSetMode
                          grSetColor
                          grMoveTo

See PrintError() function described in Appendix A

------------------------------------------------------*/

#include <stdio.h>
#include <stdlib.h>
#include <conio.h>

#include <gxlib.h>
#include <grlib.h>

void PrintError(char * funcName, int retCode);

void
main()
{
    int retValue;        /* Return value storage   */
    int dispMode;        /* 640x480x16 color       */

    /* Local initialization section */
```

```
dispMode = gxVGA_12;   /* Set up 640x480x16 colors */
retValue = 0;          /* Start clean             */

/* Mandatory kernel initialization */

retValue = gxSetDisplay(dispMode);
if(retValue < 0)
{
    PrintError("gxSetDisplay", retValue);
    return;
}

/* Let's set up our desired video mode */

retValue = gxSetMode(gxGRAPHICS);
if(retValue < 0)
{
    PrintError("gxSetMode", retValue);
    return;
}

/* Let's set the line color */

retValue = grSetColor(grYELLOW);
if(retValue < 0)
{
    PrintError("grSetColor", retValue);
    return;
}

/*
   Place cursor pointer at left edge in
   the middle of the screen
*/

retValue = grMoveTo(0, 320);
if(retValue < 0)
{
    PrintError("grMoveTo", retValue);
    return;
}

/* Draw a line in yellow */
```

```
    retValue = grLineRel(50, 75);
    if(retValue < 0)
    {
        PrintError("grLineRel", retValue);
        return;
    }

    /* Wait for a user keypress, then clean up and exit */

    getch();

    retValue = gxSetMode(gxTEXT);
    if(retValue < 0)
    {
        PrintError("gxSetMode", retValue);
        return;
    }

    return;
}
```

GRLINETO

This function draws a line from the current cursor position (CP) to the specified coordinates.

Syntax: `int far pascal grLineTo(x, y)`

Parameter: `x, y`

Type: `int`

Description: End-of-line coordinates.

Comments: This function differs from `grLineRel` because it does not draw to an offset of the cursor position; it draws to a specific coordinate position. If the CP is located at *a,b*, the line is drawn starting at *a,b* and ending at x,y; next, the CP is advanced to x,y.

Return value: Success returns `gxSUCCESS`. Failure returns an error code (negative value).

See also: `grLineRel`, `grMoveTo`, `grMoveRel`, `grOutText`

Example:

```
/*--------------------------------------------------------

Filename: grLT.C

Function: grLineTo

Description: Draws a yellow line from the current
            cursor position to the given points.
            Compare with grLineRel.

Prerequisite Function(s): gxSetDisplay
                          gxSetMode
                          grSetColor
                          grMoveTo

See PrintError() function described in Appendix A

--------------------------------------------------------*/

#include <stdio.h>
#include <stdlib.h>
#include <conio.h>

#include <gxlib.h>
#include <grlib.h>

void PrintError(char * funcName, int retCode);

void
main()
{
    int retValue;        /* Return value storage    */
    int dispMode;        /* 640x480x16 color        */

    /* Local initialization section */

    dispMode = gxVGA_12;  /* Set up 640x480x16 colors */
    retValue = 0;         /* Start clean               */

    /* Mandatory kernel initialization */

    retValue = gxSetDisplay(dispMode);
    if(retValue < 0)
```

```
    {
        PrintError("gxSetDisplay", retValue);
        return;
    }

    /* Let's set up our desired video mode */

    retValue = gxSetMode(gxGRAPHICS);
    if(retValue < 0)
    {
        PrintError("gxSetMode", retValue);
        return;
    }

    /* Let's set the line color */

    retValue = grSetColor(grYELLOW);
    if(retValue < 0)
    {
        PrintError("grSetColor", retValue);
        return;
    }

    /*
        Place cursor pointer at left edge in
        the middle of the screen
    */

    retValue = grMoveTo(0, 320);
    if(retValue < 0)
    {
        PrintError("grMoveTo", retValue);
        return;
    }

    /* Draw a line in yellow */

    retValue = grLineTo(50, 75);
    if(retValue < 0)
    {
        PrintError("grLineTo", retValue);
        return;
    }

    /* Wait for a user keypress, then clean up and exit */
```

```
getch();

retValue = gxSetMode(gxTEXT);
if(retValue < 0)
{
    PrintError("gxSetMode", retValue);
    return;
}

return;
}
```

GrMoveRel

This function moves the current cursor position (CP) to a new position relative to the specified coordinates.

Syntax: `int far pascal grMoveRel(dx, dy)`

Parameter: `dx, dy`

Type: `int`

Description: New relative CP position.

Comments: This function moves the CP to the relative coordinates. If the CP is at x, y, it is moved to $(x+dx), (y+dy)$. Note that the CP coordinates are relative to the current viewport, set by `grSetViewPort`. If you are using a viewport and want screen coordinates, add the CP's x and y coordinates to the viewport's upper-left x and y coordinates, respectively.

Return value: Success returns `gxSUCCESS`. Failure returns an error code (negative value).

See also: `grLineRel`, `grMoveTo`, `grSetViewPort`, `grOutText`

Example:
```
/*----------------------------------------------------------

Filename: grMR.C

Function: grMoveRel
```

```
Description: Moves the cursor position 50, 50, relative
             to the current cursor position, which is at
             the end of the sentence printed at 0, 100.

Prerequisite Function(s): gxSetDisplay
                          gxSetMode
                          grOutText
                          grMoveTo

See PrintError() function described in Appendix A

-------------------------------------------------------*/

#include <stdio.h>
#include <stdlib.h>
#include <conio.h>

#include <gxlib.h>
#include <grlib.h>

void PrintError(char * funcName, int retCode);

void
main()
{
    int retValue;        /* Return value storage     */
    int dispMode;        /* 640x480x16 color         */

    /* Local initialization section */

    dispMode = gxVGA_12; /* Set up 640x480x16 colors */
    retValue = 0;        /* Start clean              */

    /* Mandatory kernel initialization */

    retValue = gxSetDisplay(dispMode);
    if(retValue < 0)
    {
        PrintError("gxSetDisplay", retValue);
        return;
    }

    /* Let's set up our desired video mode */

    retValue = gxSetMode(gxGRAPHICS);
    if(retValue < 0)
```

```
{
    PrintError("gxSetMode", retValue);
    return;
}

/*
   Place cursor pointer to left edge
   of the middle of the screen
*/

retValue = grMoveTo(0, 100);
if(retValue < 0)
{
    PrintError("grMoveTo", retValue);
    return;
}

/* Print at the original location */

retValue = grOutText(
    "This is the original cursor position");
if(retValue < 0)
{
    PrintError("grOutText", retValue);
    return;
}

/* Move the cursor relative to 0,100 */

retValue = grMoveRel(50, 50);
if(retValue < 0)
{
    PrintError("grMoveRel", retValue);
    return;
}

/* Print at the new location */

retValue = grOutText(
    "This is the new cursor position");
if(retValue < 0)
{
    PrintError("grOutText", retValue);
    return;
}
```

```
    /* Get a user keypress */

    getch();

    /* Clean up and exit */

    retValue = gxSetMode(gxTEXT);
    if(retValue < 0)
    {
        PrintError("gxSetMode", retValue);
        return;
    }

    return;
}
```

grMoveTo

This function moves the current cursor position (CP) to the specified coordinates.

Syntax: `int far pascal grMoveTo(x, y)`

Parameter: x, y

Type: `int`

Description: New CP position.

Comments: This function moves the CP to the specified coordinates. Note that the CP coordinates are relative to the current viewport, set by `grSetViewPort`. If you are using a viewport and want screen coordinates, add the CP's x and y coordinates to the viewport's upper-left x and y coordinates, respectively.

Return value: Success returns `gxSUCCESS`. Failure returns an error code (negative value).

See also: `grLineRel`, `grMoveRel`, `grSetViewPort`, `grOutText`

Example:

```
/*-----------------------------------------------------

Filename: grMT.C
```

```
Function: grMoveTo

Description: Moves the cursor position to 50, 50,
             and prints a sentence there.

Prerequisite Function(s): gxSetDisplay
                          gxSetMode
                          grOutText

See PrintError() function described in Appendix A

- - - - - - - - - - - - - - - -   - - - - - - - - - - - - - - - - - - - - - - - - - - - - - - - - -*/

#include <stdio.h>
#include <stdlib.h>
#include <conio.h>

#include <gxlib.h>
#include <grlib.h>

void PrintError(char * funcName, int retCode);

void
main()
{
    int retValue;           /* Return value storage    */
    int dispMode;           /* 640x480x16 color        */

    /* Local initialization section */

    dispMode = gxVGA_12;   /* Set up 640x480x16 colors */
    retValue = 0;           /* Start clean              */

    /* Mandatory kernel initialization */

    retValue = gxSetDisplay(dispMode);
    if(retValue < 0)
    {
        PrintError("gxSetDisplay", retValue);
        return;
    }

    /* Let's set up our desired video mode */
```

```
retValue = gxSetMode(gxGRAPHICS);
if(retValue < 0)
{
    PrintError("gxSetMode", retValue);
    return;
}

/* Place cursor pointer to 50, 50 */

retValue = grMoveTo(50, 50);
if(retValue < 0)
{
    PrintError("grMoveTo", retValue);
    return;
}

/* Print at the original location */

retValue = grOutText(
    "This is the cursor position");
if(retValue < 0)
{
    PrintError("grOutText", retValue);
    return;
}

/* Get a user keypress */

getch();

/* Clean up and exit */

retValue = gxSetMode(gxTEXT);
if(retValue < 0)
{
    PrintError("gxSetMode", retValue);
    return;
}

return;
}
```

GROUTTEXT

This function displays the specified string of text at the current cursor position.

Syntax: `int far pascal grOutText(text)`

Parameter: `text`

Type: `char *`

Description: Pointer to text.

Comments: The text is displayed using the current font style, color, and justification settings. The CP does *not* advance unless the horizontal justification setting is `grTLEFT`. Note that the text strings are limited to a maximum of 127 characters.

Return value: Success returns `gxSUCCESS`. Failure returns an error code (negative value).

See also: `grGetTextStyle`, `grGetColor`, `grGetTextJustify`

Example:

```
/*-----------------------------------------------------

Filename: grOT.C

Function: grOutText

Description: Moves the cursor position to 50, 50,
            and prints a sentence there.

Prerequisite Function(s): gxSetDisplay
                          gxSetMode
                          grSetColor

See PrintError() function described in Appendix A

------------------------------------------------------*/

#include <stdio.h>
#include <stdlib.h>
#include <conio.h>
```

```
#include <gxlib.h>
#include <grlib.h>

void PrintError(char * funcName, int retCode);

void
main()
{
    int retValue;          /* Return value storage    */
    int dispMode;          /* 640x480x16 color        */

    /* Local initialization section */

    dispMode = gxVGA_12;   /* Set up 640x480x16 colors */
    retValue = 0;          /* Start clean              */

    /* Mandatory kernel initialization */

    retValue = gxSetDisplay(dispMode);
    if(retValue < 0)
    {
        PrintError("gxSetDisplay", retValue);
        return;
    }

    /* Let's set up our desired video mode */

    retValue = gxSetMode(gxGRAPHICS);
    if(retValue < 0)
    {
        PrintError("gxSetMode", retValue);
        return;
    }

    /* Set text color to red */

    retValue = grSetColor(gxRED);
    if(retValue < 0)
    {
        PrintError("grSetColor", retValue);
        return;
    }

    /* Print at 0, 0 */
```

```
retValue = grOutText("This is graphics text.");
if(retValue < 0)
{
    PrintError("grOutText", retValue);
    return;
}

/* Get a user keypress */

getch();

/* Clean up and exit */

retValue = gxSetMode(gxTEXT);
if(retValue < 0)
{
    PrintError("gxSetMode", retValue);
    return;
}

return;
}
```

GRPUTPIXEL

This function puts (places) a pixel at the specified coordinates.

Syntax: `int far pascal grPutPixel(x, y, color)`

Parameter: x, y

Type: `int`

Description: Pixel coordinates.

Parameter: `color`

Type: `int`

Description: Pixel color to use.

Comments: This function places the pixel that is using the current logical operation but *not* using the current drawing color. This is the only drawing function that does not use the current foreground color. To find the current logical operation, call the function grGetOp. To change the current logical operation, call grSetOp.

Return value: Success returns gxSUCCESS. Failure returns an error code (negative value).

See also: grGetPixel, grGetOp, grSetOp

Example:

```
/*- - - - - - - - - - - - - - - - - - - - - - - - - - - - - - - - - - - - - - - - - - - - - - - - - - - - - - - - - - -

Filename: grPP.C

Function: grPutPixel

Description: Places one yellow pixel in the center of
            the screen

Prerequisite Function(s): gxSetDisplay
                          gxSetMode

See PrintError() function described in Appendix A

- - - - - - - - - - - - - - - - - - - - - - - - - - - - - - - - - - - - - - - - - - - - - - - - - - - - - -*/

#include <stdio.h>
#include <stdlib.h>
#include <conio.h>

#include <gxlib.h>
#include <grlib.h>

void PrintError(char * funcName, int retCode);

void
main()
{
    int retValue;        /* Return value storage    */
    int dispMode;        /* 640x480x16 color        */

    /* Local initialization section */
```

```
dispMode = gxVGA_12;   /* Set up 640x480x16 colors */
retValue = 0;          /* Start clean              */

/* Mandatory kernel initialization */

retValue = gxSetDisplay(dispMode);
if(retValue < 0)
{
    PrintError("gxSetDisplay", retValue);
    return;
}

/* Let's set up our desired video mode */

retValue = gxSetMode(gxGRAPHICS);
if(retValue < 0)
{
    PrintError("gxSetMode", retValue);
    return;
}

/* Place a yellow pixel in the middle */

retValue = grPutPixel(320,240, grYELLOW);
if(retValue < 0)
{
    PrintError("grPutPixel", retValue);
    return;
}

/* Wait for user keypress, then clean up and exit */

getch();

retValue = gxSetMode(gxTEXT);
if(retValue < 0)
{
    PrintError("gxSetMode", retValue);
    return;
}

return;
}
```

GRSETACTIVEPAGE

This function sets the active graphic page, which isn't necessarily the currently viewed page, for drawing commands.

Syntax: `int far pascal grSetActivePage(page)`

Parameter: `page`

Type: `int`

Description: New active page.

Comments: This function enables you to set any page into which you draw graphics. You can draw the graphics into the active page without it being the currently viewed page but then make it the currently viewed page with a call to `gxSetPage`.

Return value: Success returns `gxSUCCESS`. Failure returns an error code (negative value).

See also: `grGetActivePage`, `gxSetPage`

Example:

```
/*------------------------------------------------------

Filename: grSAP.C

Function: grSetActivePage

Description: Returns the active page

Prerequisite Function(s): gxSetDisplay
                          gxSetMode
                          gxSetPage
                          grSetFillStyle
                          grDrawRect

See PrintError() function described in Appendix A

------------------------------------------------------*/

#include <stdio.h>
#include <stdlib.h>
#include <conio.h>
```

```
#include <gxlib.h>
#include <grlib.h>

void PrintError(char * funcName, int retCode);

void
main()
{
    int retValue;          /* Return value storage    */
    int dispMode;          /* 640x350x16 color        */

    /* Local initialization section */

    dispMode = gxEGA_10;   /* Set up 640x350x16 colors */
    retValue = 0;          /* Start clean               */

    /* Mandatory kernel initialization */

    retValue = gxSetDisplay(dispMode);
    if(retValue < 0)
    {
        PrintError("gxSetDisplay", retValue);
        return;
    }

    /* Let's set up our desired video mode */

    retValue = gxSetMode(gxGRAPHICS);
    if(retValue < 0)
    {
        PrintError("gxSetMode", retValue);
        return;
    }

    /* Make page 1 the active page */

    retValue = grSetActivePage(1);
    if(retValue < 0)
    {
        PrintError("grSetActivePage", retValue);
        return;
    }

    /*
        The fill style and color must be set
        before doing a grDrawRect
    */
```

```
retValue = grSetFillStyle(grFHATCH, grGREEN,
                          grOPAQUE);
if(retValue < 0)
{
    PrintError("grSetFillStyle", retValue);
    return;
}

/* Now we can draw into page 1 */

retValue = grDrawRect(0,0, 75,100, grFILL);
if(retValue < 0)
{
    PrintError("grDrawRect", retValue);
    return;
}

/* Get the first user keypress */

printf("Press a key to see the active drawing page
       ...\n");

getch();

/* Make page 1 the displayed page */

retValue = gxSetPage(1);
if(retValue < 0)
{
    PrintError("gxSetPage", retValue);
    return;
}

/* Get the last user keypress */

getch();

/* Clean up and exit */

retValue = gxSetMode(gxTEXT);
if(retValue < 0)
{
    PrintError("gxSetMode", retValue);
```

```
        return;
    }

    return;
}
```

GRSETBKCOLOR

This function changes the current background color to the specified value.

Syntax: `int far pascal grSetBkColor(color)`

Parameter: `color`

Type: `int`

Description: New background color.

Comments: Use this color as the background color for drawing operations such as `grClearViewPort`. Note that this is not the palette background color 0, as in the Borland Graphics Interface (BGI). This background color is an internal color that can be changed without affecting any color currently on the display. You can retrieve the current background color with a call to the function `grGetBkColor`.

Return value: Success returns `gxSUCCESS`. Failure returns an error code (negative value).

See also: `grGetBkColor, grSetColor, grSetFillStyle`

Example:

```
/*------------------------------------------------------

Filename: grSBC.C

Function: grSetBkColor

Description: Sets the background color to red, which is
            represented as the color not filled in by
            the white hatch pattern
```

```
Prerequisite Function(s): gxSetDisplay
                          gxSetMode
                          grSetFillStyle
                          grDrawRect

See PrintError() function described in Appendix A

-------------------------------------------------------*/

#include <stdio.h>
#include <stdlib.h>
#include <conio.h>

#include <gxlib.h>
#include <grlib.h>

void PrintError(char * funcName, int retCode);

void
main()
{
    int retValue;        /* Return value storage    */
    int dispMode;        /* 640x350x16 color        */

    /* Local initialization section */

    dispMode = gxEGA_10;  /* Set up 640x350x16 colors */
    retValue = 0;         /* Start clean              */

    /* Mandatory kernel initialization */

    retValue = gxSetDisplay(dispMode);
    if(retValue < 0)
    {
        PrintError("gxSetDisplay", retValue);
        return;
    }

    /* Let's set up our desired video mode */

    retValue = gxSetMode(gxGRAPHICS);
    if(retValue < 0)
    {
        PrintError("gxSetMode", retValue);
        return;
    }
```

```
/*
   The fill style and color must be set
   before doing a grDrawRect
*/

retValue = grSetFillStyle(grFHATCH, grWHITE,
                          grOPAQUE);
if(retValue < 0)
{
    PrintError("grSetFillStyle", retValue);
    return;
}

/* Set the background color to red */

retValue = grSetBkColor(grRED);
if(retValue < 0)
{
    PrintError("grSetBkColor", retValue);
    return;
}

retValue = grDrawRect(0,0, 100,100,
                      grFILL+grOUTLINE);
if(retValue < 0)
{
    PrintError("grDrawRect", retValue);
    return;
}

/* Get user keypress */

getch();

/* Clean up and exit */

retValue = gxSetMode(gxTEXT);
if(retValue < 0)
{
    PrintError("gxSetMode", retValue);
    return;
}

return;
}
```

GRSETCLIPPING

This function sets the clipping status.

Syntax: `int far pascal grSetClipping(clipFlag)`

Parameter: `clipFlag`

Type: `int`

Description: `grCLIP` or `grNOCLIP`.

Comments: `grCLIP` enables clipping, and `grNOCLIP` disables clipping. The clipping status determines whether drawing commands are clipped at the clipping region defined by `grSetClipRegion`. This function does *not* set the coordinates at which clipping occurs: it only defines *if* clipping will occur. See `grSetClipRegion` to change the clipping coordinates. Make sure you call `grSetClipRegion` to set up clipping coordinates before calling this function, or else you will get unexpected results.

Return value: Success returns `gxSUCCESS`. Failure returns an error code (negative value).

See also: `grSetClipRegion`, `grGetClipRegion`, `grGetClipping`

Example:

```
/*--------------------------------------------------------

Filename: grSCL.C

Function: grSetClipping

Description: Sets the clipping region coordinates,
            enables clipping, and draws a blue outline
            square. The upper and left edges will be
            clipped.

Prerequisite Function(s): gxSetDisplay
                          gxSetMode
                          grSetClipRegion
                          grDrawSquare
```

See PrintError() function described in Appendix A

```
----------------------------------------------------*/

#include <stdio.h>
#include <stdlib.h>
#include <conio.h>

#include <gxlib.h>
#include <grlib.h>

void PrintError(char * funcName, int retCode);

void
main()
{
    int retValue;          /* Return value storage      */
    int dispMode;          /* 640x480x16 color          */

    /* Local initialization section */

    dispMode = gxVGA_12;   /* Set up 640x480x16 colors */
    retValue = 0;          /* Start clean               */

    /* Mandatory kernel initialization */

    retValue = gxSetDisplay(dispMode);
    if(retValue < 0)
    {
        PrintError("gxSetDisplay", retValue);
        return;
    }

    /* Let's set up our desired video mode */

    retValue = gxSetMode(gxGRAPHICS);
    if(retValue < 0)
    {
        PrintError("gxSetMode", retValue);
        return;
    }

    /* Set the clipping region */
```

```
retValue = grSetClipRegion(20,20, 100,100);
if(retValue < 0)
{
    PrintError("grSetClipRegion", retValue);
    return;
}

/* Enable Clipping */

retValue = grSetClipping(grCLIP);
if(retValue < 0)
{
    PrintError("grSetClipping", retValue);
    return;
}

/* Draw an outline square */

retValue = grDrawSquare(0,0, 50, grOUTLINE);
if(retValue < 0)
{
    PrintError("grDrawSquare", retValue);
    return;
}

/* Wait for a user keypress, then clean up and exit */

getch();

retValue = gxSetMode(gxTEXT);
if(retValue < 0)
{
    PrintError("gxSetMode", retValue);
    return;
}

return;
}
```

GRSETCLIPREGION

This function sets a new clipping coordinate region to the specified values.

Syntax: `int far pascal grSetClipRegion(x1, x2, y1, y2)`

Parameter: `x1, y1`

Type: `int`

Description: New upper-right corner coordinates of clip region.

Parameter: `x2, y2`

Type: `int`

Description: New lower-left corner coordinates of clip region.

Comments: Any part of a graphic or image being drawn that falls out of this coordinate boundary is clipped (not displayed). This function does *not* enable the clipping feature: it only sets up the coordinates used for clipping when clipping is enabled. Call the function `grSetClipping` to enable and disable clipping. Make sure you call this function to set up the clipping coordinates before you call `grSetClipping`, or you will get unexpected results.

Return value: Success returns `gxSUCCESS`. Failure returns an error code (negative value).

See also: `grSetClipRegion`, `grGetClipRegion`, `grGetClipping`

Example:

```
/*------------------------------------------------------

Filename: grSCR.C

Function: grSetClipRegion

Description: Sets the clipping region coordinates. See
            grSetClipping for a clipping example

Prerequisite Function(s): gxSetDisplay
                          gxSetMode

See PrintError() function described in Appendix A

-------------------------------------------------------*/
```

```c
#include <stdio.h>
#include <stdlib.h>
#include <conio.h>

#include <gxlib.h>
#include <grlib.h>

void PrintError(char * funcName, int retCode);

void
main()
{
    int retValue;        /* Return value storage     */
    int dispMode;        /* 640x480x16 color         */

    /* Local initialization section */

    dispMode = gxVGA_12;  /* Set up 640x480x16 colors */
    retValue = 0;         /* Start clean               */

    /* Mandatory kernel initialization */

    retValue = gxSetDisplay(dispMode);
    if(retValue < 0)
    {
        PrintError("gxSetDisplay", retValue);
        return;
    }

    /* Let's set up our desired video mode */

    retValue = gxSetMode(gxGRAPHICS);
    if(retValue < 0)
    {
        PrintError("gxSetMode", retValue);
        return;
    }

    /* Set the clipping region */

    retValue = grSetClipRegion(20,20, 100,100);
    if(retValue < 0)
    {
        PrintError("grSetClipRegion", retValue);
        return;
    }
```

```
/* Wait for user keypress, then clean up and exit */

printf("Clipping region has been set ...\n");

getch();

retValue = gxSetMode(gxTEXT);
if(retValue < 0)
{
    PrintError("gxSetMode", retValue);
    return;
}

return;
}
```

GRSETCOLOR

This function changes the drawing color used for all drawing operations to the specified value.

Syntax: `int far pascal grSetColor(color)`

Parameter: `color`

Type: `int`

Description: New foreground (drawing) color.

Comments: Use this color when plotting pixels, lines, circles, and all other drawing operations. This color is not a fill color for rectangles, squares, and so on, but is for drawing lines, and outlines of rectangles, squares, etc. (See the function `grSetFillStyle` to change the fill color.) The color can be one of the predefined constants (found in Appendix A) or a direct color value. The actual colors displayed vary depending on the current display palette. Call the function `grGetColor` to retrieve the current drawing color. To see how this function affects line drawing and fill routines, check the table on the function page for `grDrawRect`.

Return value: Success returns gxSUCCESS. Failure returns an error code (negative value).

See also: grGetColor

Example:

```
/*----------------------------------------------------------

Filename: grSC.C

Function: grSetColor

Description: Sets the current foreground color, which is
            represented here as the outline for a
            rectangle

Prerequisite Function(s): gxSetDisplay
                          gxSetMode
                          grSetFillStyle
                          grDrawRect

See PrintError() function described in Appendix A

----------------------------------------------------------*/

#include <stdio.h>
#include <stdlib.h>
#include <conio.h>

#include <gxlib.h>
#include <grlib.h>

void PrintError(char * funcName, int retCode);

void
main()
{
    int retValue;           /* Return value storage    */
    int dispMode;           /* 640x350x16 color        */

    /* Local initialization section */

    dispMode = gxEGA_10;    /* Set up 640x350x16 colors */
    retValue = 0;           /* Start clean               */
```

```
/* Mandatory kernel initialization */

retValue = gxSetDisplay(dispMode);
if(retValue < 0)
{
    PrintError("gxSetDisplay", retValue);
    return;
}

/* Let's set up our desired video mode */

retValue = gxSetMode(gxGRAPHICS);
if(retValue < 0)
{
    PrintError("gxSetMode", retValue);
    return;
}

/*
   The fill style and color must be set
   before doing a grDrawRect
*/

retValue = grSetFillStyle(grFHATCH, grWHITE,
                          grOPAQUE);
if(retValue < 0)
{
    PrintError("grSetFillStyle", retValue);
    return;
}

/* Set the foreground color to red */

retValue = grSetColor(grRED);
if(retValue < 0)
{
    PrintError("grSetColor", retValue);
    return;
}

retValue = grDrawRect(0,0, 100,100,
                      grFILL+grOUTLINE);
if(retValue < 0)
```

```
{
    PrintError("grDrawRect", retValue);
    return;
}

/* Get user keypress */

getch();

/* Clean up and exit */

retValue = gxSetMode(gxTEXT);
if(retValue < 0)
{
    PrintError("gxSetMode", retValue);
    return;
}

return;
}
```

GRSETFILLPATTERN

This function changes the current fill pattern to the specified pattern.

Syntax: `int far pascal grSetFillPattern(style, pattern)`

Parameter: `style`

Type: `int`

Description: Fill style of new pattern.

Parameter: `pattern`

Type: `char *`

Description: Pointer to new pattern data.

Comments: The buffer should be eight bytes (for example, `char pattern[8]`). The eight bits in each byte of the array represent one horizontal line of eight pixels. Therefore, the fill pattern is an 8x8

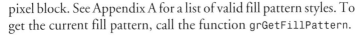
pixel block. See Appendix A for a list of valid fill pattern styles. To get the current fill pattern, call the function grGetFillPattern.

Return value: Success returns gxSUCCESS. Failure returns an error code (negative value).

See also: grGetFillPattern, grGetFillStyle

Example:

```
/*-------------------------------------------------------

Filename: grSFP.C

Function: grSetFillPattern

Description: Creates a new pattern (diamonds), and makes
             it current for the grFUSER format

Prerequisite Function(s): gxSetDisplay
                          gxSetMode

See PrintError() function described in Appendix A

-----------------------------------------------------*/

#include <stdio.h>
#include <stdlib.h>
#include <conio.h>

#include <gxlib.h>
#include <grlib.h>

void PrintError(char * funcName, int retCode);

/* Globals variables here... */

char fillPattern[8];

void
main()
{
    int retValue;        /* Return value storage    */
    int dispMode;        /* 640x480x16 color        */

    /* Local initialization section */
```

```
dispMode = gxVGA_12;   /* Set up 640x480x16 colors */
retValue = 0;          /* Start clean             */

/* Mandatory kernel initialization */

retValue = gxSetDisplay(dispMode);
if(retValue < 0)
{
    PrintError("gxSetDisplay", retValue);
    return;
}

/* Let's set up our desired video mode */

retValue = gxSetMode(gxGRAPHICS);
if(retValue < 0)
{
    PrintError("gxSetMode", retValue);
    return;
}

/* Let's make the background color blue */

retValue = grSetBkColor(gxBLUE);
if(retValue < 0)
{
    PrintError("grSetBkColor", retValue);
    return;
}

/* Make a diamond pattern */
fillPattern[0] = 0x20;
fillPattern[1] = 0x50;
fillPattern[2] = 0x88;
fillPattern[3] = 0x50;
fillPattern[4] = 0x20;
fillPattern[5] = 0x00;
fillPattern[6] = 0x00;
fillPattern[7] = 0x00;

/* Use the grFUSER fill style position */

retValue = grSetFillPattern(grFUSER, fillPattern);
if(retValue < 0)
```

```
{
    PrintError("grSetFillPattern", retValue);
    return;
}

/* Set the fill style and color */

retValue = grSetFillStyle(grFUSER, grWHITE,
                          grOPAQUE);
if(retValue < 0)
{
    PrintError("grSetFillStyle", retValue);
    return;
}

/* Draw a rectangle, using the new fill style */

retValue = grDrawRect(0,0, 400,400, grFILL);
if(retValue < 0)
{
    PrintError("grDrawRect", retValue);
    return;
}

/* Wait for a user keypress, then clean up and exit */

getch();

retValue = gxSetMode(gxTEXT);
if(retValue < 0)
{
    PrintError("gxSetMode", retValue);
    return;
}

    return;
}
```

GRSETFILLSTYLE

This function changes the current fill pattern style, color, and transparency to the specified values.

Syntax: `int far pascal grSetFillStyle(style, color, trans)`

Parameter: `style`

Type: `int`

Description: New fill style setting.

Parameter: `color`

Type: `int`

Description: New fill color.

Parameter: `trans`

Type: `int`

Description: New transparency setting.

Comments: You can retrieve the current fill style settings by calling the function `grGetFillStyle`. See Appendix A for a list of the available fill pattern styles and colors. The transparency style is either the constant `grTRANS` or `grOPAQUE`. To see how this function affects line drawing and fill routines, check the table on the function page for `grDrawRect`.

Return value: Success returns `gxSUCCESS`. Failure returns an error code (negative value).

See also: `grGetFillPattern`, `grGetFillStyle`, `grSetFillPattern`

Example:

```
/*-------------------------------------------------------

Filename: grSFS.C

Function: grSetFillStyle

Description: Sets new fill style, color, and trans-
             parency, and draws a rectangle to show it
```

```
Prerequisite Function(s): gxSetDisplay
                          gxSetMode

See PrintError() function described in Appendix A

-----------------------------------------------------*/

#include <stdio.h>
#include <stdlib.h>
#include <conio.h>

#include <gxlib.h>
#include <grlib.h>

void PrintError(char * funcName, int retCode);

void
main()
{
    int retValue;       /* Return value storage    */
    int dispMode;       /* 640x480x16 color        */

    /* Local initialization section */

    dispMode = gxVGA_12; /* Set up 640x480x16 colors */
    retValue = 0;        /* Start clean              */

    /* Mandatory kernel initialization */

    retValue = gxSetDisplay(dispMode);
    if(retValue < 0)
    {
        PrintError("gxSetDisplay", retValue);
        return;
    }

    /* Let's set up our desired video mode */

    retValue = gxSetMode(gxGRAPHICS);
    if(retValue < 0)
    {
        PrintError("gxSetMode", retValue);
        return;
    }
```

```
/*
    Set the fill style, color, and
    transparency type
*/

retValue = grSetFillStyle(grFHATCH, grBLUE,
                          grOPAQUE);
if(retValue < 0)
{
    PrintError("grSetFillStyle", retValue);
    return;
}

/*
    Draw a rectangle to show what it
    looks like
*/

retValue = grDrawRect(0,0, 75,100, grFILL);
if(retValue < 0)
{
    PrintError("grDrawRect", retValue);
    return;
}

/* Wait for a user keypress, then clean up and exit */

getch();

retValue = gxSetMode(gxTEXT);
if(retValue < 0)
{
    PrintError("gxSetMode", retValue);
    return;
}

return;
}
```

GrSetLineStyle

This function changes the current line style pattern and thickness to the specified values.

Syntax: `int far pascal grSetLineStyle(style, thickness)`

Parameter: `style`

Type: `int`

Description: New line style setting.

Parameter: `thickness`

Type: `int`

Description: New line thickness.

Comments: You can retrieve the current fill style settings by calling the function `grGetLineStyle`. The line style is a 16-bit value representing 16 horizontal pixels—if the bit is set, the pixel is drawn. See Appendix A for a list of predefined line styles. You are not limited to these values: you can create your own custom line styles. The thickness value represents line thickness in pixels. Its value has no real restriction, but be careful to avoid confusion. To see how this function affects line drawing and fill routines, check the table on the function page for `grDrawRect`.

Return value: Success returns `gxSUCCESS`. Failure returns an error code (negative value).

See also: `grGetFillPattern`, `grGetFillStyle`, `grSetFillPattern`

Example:

```
/*--------------------------------------------------

Filename: grSLS.C

Function: grSetLineStyle

Description: Sets the line style and thickness. See
            grGetLineStyle for a retreival of these
            changes

Prerequisite Function(s): gxSetDisplay
```

```
    See PrintError() function described in Appendix A

    ------------------------------------------------------*/

    #include <stdio.h>
    #include <stdlib.h>
    #include <conio.h>

    #include <gxlib.h>
    #include <grlib.h>

    void PrintError(char * funcName, int retCode);

    void
    main()
    {
        int retValue;          /* Return value storage    */
        int dispMode;          /* 640x480x16 color        */

        /* Local initialization section */

        dispMode = gxVGA_12;   /* Set up 640x480x16 colors */
        retValue = 0;          /* Start clean             */

        /* Mandatory kernel initialization */

        retValue = gxSetDisplay(dispMode);
        if(retValue < 0)
        {
            PrintError("gxSetDisplay", retValue);
            return;
        }

        /* Set the line style to arbitrary values */

        retValue = grSetLineStyle(0xF5C4, 3);
        if(retValue < 0)
        {
            PrintError("grSetLineStyle", retValue);
            return;
        }

        printf("Line style has been set.\n");

        return;
    }
```

grSetMouseMask

This function sets the mouse cursor and mask for a given mouse style.

Syntax: int far pascal grSetMouseMask(style, hotx, hoty, cursor, mask)

Parameter: style

Type: int

Description: Mouse style for which to set masks.

Parameter: hotx, hoty

Type: int

Description: Location of mouse cursor hotspot.

Parameter: cursor

Type: int *

Description: Location of mouse cursor array.

Parameter: mask

Type: int

Description: Location of mouse mask array.

Comments: For a given mouse style, this function sets the mouse cursor masks into the 16-word buffers pointed to by cursor and mask. Each word in the pattern corresponds to 16 pixels. Whenever a bit in a mask byte is 1, the pixel will be plotted. The hotspot coordinates returned represent the cursor's hotspot location (the tip of the arrow, middle of the crosshair, and so on).

Return value: Success returns gxSUCCESS. Failure returns an error code (negative value).

See also: grSetMousePos

Example:

```
/*-----------------------------------------------------------

Filename: grSMM.C

Function: grSetMouseMask

Description: Sets the mouse mask for mouse grCUSER, and
            prints the mask in binary format

Prerequisite Function(s): gxSetDisplay

See PrintError() function described in Appendix A

-----------------------------------------------------------*/

#include <stdio.h>
#include <stdlib.h>
#include <conio.h>

#include <gxlib.h>
#include <grlib.h>

void PrintError(char * funcName, int retCode);

/* Globals variables here... */

int  amask[16] = {0xFE00,0xFC00,0xF800,0xF000,
                  0xE000,0xC000,0x8000,0x0000,0x0000,
                  0x0001,0x0003,0x0007,0x000F,0x001F,
                  0xFFFF,0xFFFF};
int  acurs[16] = {0x0000,0x01FE,0x0202,0x0402,0x08FE,
                  0x11FE,0x2302,0x4602,0x47E2,0x47C4,
                  0x4008,0x4010,0x7FE0,0x0000,0x0000,
                  0x0000};
void
main()
{
    int retValue;        /* Return value storage    */
    int cnt;             /* General purpose counters */
```

```
int dispMode;         /* 640x480x16 color         */
char gBuf[20];        /* General purpose buffer   */

/* Local initialization section */

dispMode = gxVGA_12;  /* Set up 640x480x16 colors */
retValue = 0;         /* Start clean              */

/* Mandatory kernel initialization */

retValue = gxSetDisplay(dispMode);
if(retValue < 0)
{
    PrintError("gxSetDisplay", retValue);
    return;
}

/*
   Set the bytes for the grCUSER cursor style to the
   Genus 'G'.
*/

retValue = grSetMouseMask(grCUSER, 8, 8, acurs,
                          amask);
if(retValue < 0)
{
    PrintError("grSetMouseMask", retValue);
    return;
}

/*
   Set the mouse style to the new user type,
   and the color to blue.
*/

retValue = grSetMouseStyle(grCUSER, grBLUE);
if(retValue < 0)
{
    PrintError("grSetMouseStyle", retValue);
    return;
}
else
{
    printf("grCUSER successfully mouse style
            set.\n");
}
```

```
/*
   To use this cursor, remember that you still have
   to call grInitMouse and grDisplayMouse. See the
   grSetMouseStyle example for more information ...
*/


/*
   Print the cursor and the mask in binary format
*/

printf("The cursor for grCUSER is:    ");
printf("The mask   for grCUSER is:\n\n");

for(cnt=0; cnt<16; cnt++)
{
   (void) itoa((unsigned int)acurs[cnt], gBuf, 2);
   printf("    %016s          ", gBuf, gBuf);

   (void) itoa((unsigned int)amask[cnt], gBuf, 2);
   printf("    %016s\n", gBuf, gBuf);
}
printf("\n\n");

   return;
}
```

GRSETMOUSEPOS

This function moves the mouse to the specified position.

Syntax: `int far pascal grSetMousePos(x, y)`

Parameter: x, y

Type: int

Description: New mouse position.

Comments: The coordinates for this function are always screen coordinates. This function moves the cursor anywhere on the screen, even if automatic mouse tracking is enabled (see grTrackMouse). You can call this function even if the mouse cursor is hidden.

Return value: Success returns gxSUCCESS. Failure returns an error code (negative value).

See also: grGetMousePos

Example:

```
/*-----------------------------------------------------------

Filename: grSMP.C

Function: grSetMousePos

Description: Displays the mouse, waits for a keypress,
            and sets the mouse position

Prerequisite Function(s): gxSetDisplay
                          gxSetMode
                          grInitMouse
                          grTrackMouse
                          grStopMouse
                          grDisplayMouse

See PrintError() function described in Appendix A

-----------------------------------------------------------*/

#include <stdio.h>
#include <stdlib.h>
#include <conio.h>

#include <gxlib.h>
#include <grlib.h>

void PrintError(char * funcName, int retCode);

void
main()
{
    int retValue;       /* Return value storage   */
    int dispMode;       /* 640x480x16 color       */

    /* Local initialization section */

    dispMode = gxVGA_12;  /* Set up 640x480x16 colors */
    retValue = 0;         /* Start clean              */
```

```c
/* Mandatory kernel initialization */

retValue = gxSetDisplay(dispMode);
if(retValue < 0)
{
    PrintError("gxSetDisplay", retValue);
    return;
}

/* Let's set up our desired video mode */

retValue = gxSetMode(gxGRAPHICS);
if(retValue < 0)
{
    PrintError("gxSetMode", retValue);
    return;
}

/* Initialize and install mouse driver */

retValue = grInitMouse();
if(retValue < 0)
{
    PrintError("grInitMouse", retValue);
    return;
}

/* Track the mouse movement */

retValue = grTrackMouse(grTRACK);
if(retValue < 0)
{
    PrintError("grTrackMouse", retValue);
    return;
}

/* Turn the mouse on */

retValue = grDisplayMouse(grSHOW);
if(retValue < 0)
{
    PrintError("grDisplayMouse", retValue);
    return;
}
```

```
/*
   Set the mouse to near the bottom
   corner of the screen
*/

printf("To set mouse position to the bottom corner, ");
printf("press any key.\n");

getch();

retValue = grSetMousePos(620, 460);
if(retValue < 0)
{
    PrintError("grSetMousePos", retValue);
    return;
}

/* Wait for a user keypress */

printf("Now press any key to exit ...\n");

getch();

/* Turn the mouse off */

retValue = grDisplayMouse(grHIDE);
if(retValue < 0)
{
    PrintError("grDisplayMouse", retValue);
    return;
}

/* De-init and remove mouse driver */

retValue = grStopMouse();
if(retValue < 0)
{
    PrintError("grStopMouse", retValue);
    return;
}

/* Return to text mode */
```

```
    retValue = gxSetMode(gxTEXT);
    if(retValue < 0)
    {
        PrintError("gxSetMode", retValue);
        return;
    }

    return;
}
```

GRSETMOUSESTYLE

This function changes the current mouse style and color to the specified values.

Syntax: `int far pascal grSetMouseStyle(style, color)`

Parameter: `style`

Type: `int`

Description: New mouse style.

Parameter: `color`

Type: `int`

Description: New mouse color.

Comments: See Appendix A for a list of valid mouse styles and colors.

Return value: Success returns `gxSUCCESS`. Failure returns an error code (negative value).

See also: `grGetMouseStyle`

Example:

```
/*------------------------------------------------------

Filename: grSMS.C

Function: grSetMouseStyle
```

```
Description: Sets the mouse style to an hourglass, and
            the color to red

Prerequisite Function(s): gxSetDisplay
                          gxSetMode

See PrintError() function described in Appendix A

------------------------------------------------------*/

#include <stdio.h>
#include <stdlib.h>
#include <conio.h>

#include <gxlib.h>
#include <grlib.h>

void PrintError(char * funcName, int retCode);

void
main()
{
    int retValue;        /* Return value storage    */
    int dispMode;        /* 640x480x16 color        */

    /* Local initialization section */

    dispMode = gxVGA_12; /* Set up 640x480x16 colors */
    retValue = 0;        /* Start clean               */

    /* Mandatory kernel initialization */

    retValue = gxSetDisplay(dispMode);
    if(retValue < 0)
    {
        PrintError("gxSetDisplay", retValue);
        return;
    }

    /* Let's set up our desired video mode */

    retValue = gxSetMode(gxGRAPHICS);
    if(retValue < 0)
    {
        PrintError("gxSetMode", retValue);
        return;
    }
```

```
/* Initialize and install mouse driver */

retValue = grInitMouse();
if(retValue < 0)
{
    PrintError("grInitMouse", retValue);
    return;
}

/* Track the mouse movement */

retValue = grTrackMouse(grTRACK);
if(retValue < 0)
{
    PrintError("grTrackMouse", retValue);
    return;
}

/* Turn the mouse on */

retValue = grDisplayMouse(grSHOW);
if(retValue < 0)
{
    PrintError("grDisplayMouse", retValue);
    return;
}

/* Loop, waiting for a mouse button press */

printf("Press a mouse button to change mouse
        style.\n");

while(!(retValue = grGetMouseButtons()));

/*
    Set the mouse style to an hourglass,
    and the color to red.
*/

retValue = grSetMouseStyle(grCTIME, grRED);
if(retValue < 0)
{
    PrintError("grSetMouseStyle", retValue);
    return;
}
```

```
/* Waiting for a keypress */

printf("Press any key to exit ...\n");

getch();

/* Return to text mode */

retValue = gxSetMode(gxTEXT);
if(retValue < 0)
{
    PrintError("gxSetMode", retValue);
    return;
}

    return;
}
```

GRSETOP

This function sets the logical operation to the specified value.

Syntax: `int far pascal grSetOp(op)`

Parameter: `op`

Type: `int`

Description: New logical (bitwise) operation.

Comments: The most common logical operation is `gxSET`—replace all pixels with the pattern or image being drawn. The other operations available are `gxAND`, `gxOR`, and `gxXOR`. You can use the `gxXOR` operation to draw rubber-banding lines and rectangles. Simply draw the line using `gxXOR` as the operation; then draw it again to remove it. You do not need to save the data underneath the line.

Return value: Success returns `gxSUCCESS`. Failure returns an error code (negative value).

See also: `grGetOp`, `gxPutImage`

Example:

```
/*----------------------------------------------------

Filename: grSO.C

Function: grSetOp

Description: Sets the logical operation to gxXOR

Prerequisite Function(s): gxSetDisplay

See PrintError() function described in Appendix A

----------------------------------------------------*/

#include <stdio.h>
#include <stdlib.h>
#include <conio.h>

#include <gxlib.h>
#include <grlib.h>

void PrintError(char * funcName, int retCode);

void
main()
{
    int retValue;          /* Return value storage    */
    int dispMode;          /* 640x480x16 color        */

    /* Local initialization section */

    dispMode = gxVGA_12;   /* Set up 640x480x16 colors */
    retValue = 0;          /* Start clean              */

    /* Mandatory kernel initialization */

    retValue = gxSetDisplay(dispMode);
    if(retValue < 0)
    {
        PrintError("gxSetDisplay", retValue);
        return;
    }

    /* Set the logical operation to AND */
```

```
retValue = grSetOp(gxAND);
if(retValue < 0)
{
    PrintError("grSetOp", retValue);
    return;
}

printf("Logical operation has been set to
        gxAND.\n");

return;
}
```

GRSETSTATE

This function changes the current graphics state to the new specified state.

Syntax: `int far pascal grSetState(state)`

Parameter: `state`

Type: `GRSTATE *`

Description: New graphics state settings.

Comments: You can retrieve the current graphics state settings by calling the function `grGetState`. This function enables you to change the current state to a new one, or reset a previously saved state back to its original setting (retrieved with a `grGetState` call). See Appendix A for a list of the `GRSTATE` structure.

Return value: Success returns `gxSUCCESS`. Failure returns an error code (negative value).

See also: `grGetState`

Example:

```
/*------------------------------------------------------

Filename: grSS.C

Function: grSetState
```

```
   Description: Sets the foreground color through
               grSetState

   Prerequisite Function(s): gxSetDisplay

   See PrintError() function described in Appendix A

   ------------------------------------------------------*/

#include <stdio.h>
#include <stdlib.h>
#include <conio.h>

#include <gxlib.h>
#include <grlib.h>

void PrintError(char * funcName, int retCode);

/* Global variables here... */

GRSTATE graphicsState;

void
main()
{
    int retValue;          /* Return value storage      */
    int dispMode;          /* 640x350x16 color          */

    /* Local initialization section */

    dispMode = gxEGA_10;  /* Set up 640x350x16 colors */
    retValue = 0;          /* Start clean               */

    /* Mandatory kernel initialization */

    retValue = gxSetDisplay(dispMode);
    if(retValue < 0)
    {
        PrintError("gxSetDisplay", retValue);
        return;
    }

    /* Get the current graphics state */
```

```
retValue = grGetState(&graphicsState);
if(retValue < 0)
{
    PrintError("gxSetDisplay", retValue);
    return;
}

/* Change the foreground color to red */

graphicsState.color = grRED;

/* Make the change */

retValue = grSetState(&graphicsState);
if(retValue < 0)
{
    PrintError("gxSetDisplay", retValue);
    return;
}
else
{
  printf("State has been changed.\n");
}

return;
}
```

GRSETTEXTJUSTIFY

This function changes the current text justification setting to the specified value.

Syntax: `int far pascal grSetTextJustify(hJust, vJust)`

Parameter: `hJust`

Type: `int`

Description: New horizontal justification setting.

Parameter: `vJust`

Type: `int`

Description: New vertical justification setting.

Comments: The justification controls placement of text displayed with grOutText. See the following list for valid justification codes.

Direction	Justification Code	Justify
Horizontal	grTLEFT	Left-Justify
Horizontal	grTCENTER	Center
Horizontal	grTRIGHT	Right-Justify
Vertical	grTTOP	Top-Justify
Vertical	grTCENTER	Center (middle)
Vertical	grTBOTTOM	Bottom-Justify

Return value: Success returns gxSUCCESS. Failure returns an error code (negative value).

See also: grGetTextJustify, grOutText

Example:

```
/*-----------------------------------------------------------

Filename: grSTJ.C

Function: grSetTextJustify

Description: Sets text justify to center/center, then
            prints sample text on the screen. The text
            will be centered horizontally.

Prerequisite Function(s): gxSetDisplay
                          gxSetMode
                          grOutText
                          grMoveTo

See PrintError() function described in Appendix A

-----------------------------------------------------*/
```

```
#include <stdio.h>
#include <stdlib.h>
#include <conio.h>

#include <gxlib.h>
#include <grlib.h>

void PrintError(char * funcName, int retCode);

void
main()
{
    int retValue;          /* Return value storage    */
    int dispMode;          /* 640x480x16 color        */

    /* Local initialization section */

    dispMode = gxVGA_12;   /* Set up 640x480x16 colors */
    retValue = 0;          /* Start clean              */

    /* Mandatory kernel initialization */

    retValue = gxSetDisplay(dispMode);
    if(retValue < 0)
    {
        PrintError("gxSetDisplay", retValue);
        return;
    }

    /* Let's set up our desired video mode */

    retValue = gxSetMode(gxGRAPHICS);
    if(retValue < 0)
    {
        PrintError("gxSetMode", retValue);
        return;
    }

    /* Set the justification to be center/top */

    retValue = grSetTextJustify(grTCENTER, grTTOP);
    if(retValue < 0)
    {
        PrintError("grSetTextJustify", retValue);
        return;
    }
```

```
/* Place cursor pointer to middle of top row */

retValue = grMoveTo(320, 0);
if(retValue < 0)
{
    PrintError("grMoveTo", retValue);
    return;
}

/*
   Print a simple message. The location will
   be centered on the top line of the screen,
   and in the default color blue
*/

retValue = grOutText(
    "This is horizontally centered text");
if(retValue < 0)
{
    PrintError("grOutText", retValue);
    return;
}

/* Get a user keypress */

getch();

/* Clean up and exit */

retValue = gxSetMode(gxTEXT);
if(retValue < 0)
{
    PrintError("gxSetMode", retValue);
    return;
}

    return;
}
```

GRSETTEXTSTYLE

This function changes the current text ROM font style and transparency setting to the specified values.

Syntax: `int far pascal grSetTextStyle(style, trans)`

Parameter: style

Type: int

Description: New text style.

Parameter: trans

Type: int

Description: New text transparency.

Comments: The font style is the one used for all text output using grOutText. See the following list for valid font and transparency settings.

Text Style Code	Font Type
grTXT8X8	ROM 8x8 font
grTXT8X14	ROM 8x14 font
grTXT8X16	ROM 8x16 font

Transparency Code	Setting
grTRANS	Transparent (no background)
grOPAQUE	Opaque text (display background)

Return value: Success returns gxSUCCESS. Failure returns an error code (negative value).

See also: grSetTextStyle, grOutText

Example:

```
/*-----------------------------------------------------

Filename: grSTS.C

Function: grSetTextStyle
```

```
Description: Sets the text style to an 8x14 font, then
             prints a sample text in the font

Prerequisite Function(s): gxSetDisplay
                          gxSetMode
                          grOutText

See PrintError() function described in Appendix A

---------------------------------------------------------*/

#include <stdio.h>
#include <stdlib.h>
#include <conio.h>

#include <gxlib.h>
#include <grlib.h>

void PrintError(char * funcName, int retCode);

void
main()
{
    int retValue;        /* Return value storage     */
    int dispMode;        /* 640x480x16 color         */

    /* Local initialization section */

    dispMode = gxVGA_12;  /* Set up 640x480x16 colors */
    retValue = 0;         /* Start clean              */

    /* Mandatory kernel initialization */

    retValue = gxSetDisplay(dispMode);
    if(retValue < 0)
    {
        PrintError("gxSetDisplay", retValue);
        return;
    }

    /* Let's set up our desired video mode */

    retValue = gxSetMode(gxGRAPHICS);
    if(retValue < 0)
    {
        PrintError("gxSetMode", retValue);
```

```
        return;
}

/* Set the font to be 8x14, transparent */

retValue = grSetTextStyle(grTXT8X14, grTRANS);
if(retValue < 0)
{
    PrintError("grSetTextStyle", retValue);
    return;
}

retValue = grSetColor(gxYELLOW);
if(retValue < 0)
{
    PrintError("grSetColor", retValue);
    return;
}

/*
    Print a simple message. The location will
    be at 0,0, in yellow.
*/

retValue = grOutText("This is an 8x14 font.");
if(retValue < 0)
{
    PrintError("grOutText", retValue);
    return;
}

/* Get a user keypress */

getch();

/* Clean up and exit */

retValue = gxSetMode(gxTEXT);
if(retValue < 0)
{
    PrintError("gxSetMode", retValue);
    return;
}

    return;
}
```

GRSETVIEWPORT

This function changes the current viewport coordinate settings to the specified coordinates.

Syntax: `int far pascal grSetViewPort(x1, y1, x2, y2)`

Parameter: x1, y1

Type: `int`

Description: New upper-left corner coordinates of viewport.

Parameter: x2, y2

Type: `int`

Description: New lower-right corner coordinates of viewport.

Comments: The viewport can act as a window, allowing drawing functions to take place with respect to the viewport's coordinates, without concern for the exact screen coordinates.

Return value: Success returns gxSUCCESS. Failure returns an error code (negative value).

See also: `grGetViewPort`

Example:

```
/*-------------------------------------------------------

Filename: grSVP.C

Function: grSetViewPort

Description: Sets the current viewport coordinates
             to the lower-right quadrant of the screen
             and draws a hatch pattern at 0,0 of the
             viewport coordinates

Prerequisite Function(s): gxSetDisplay
                          gxSetMode
                          grSetFillStyle
                          grDrawRect
```

```
See PrintError() function described in Appendix A

------------------------------------------------------*/

#include <stdio.h>
#include <stdlib.h>
#include <conio.h>

#include <gxlib.h>
#include <grlib.h>

void PrintError(char * funcName, int retCode);

void
main()
{
    int retValue;       /* Return value storage    */
    int dispMode;       /* 640x480x16 color        */
    int dispColor;      /* Display Color           */
    int dispPage;       /* Display Page            */

    /* Local initialization section */

    dispMode = gxVGA_12;  /* Set up 640x480x16 colors */
    dispColor = gxRED;    /* Do a full red screen     */
    dispPage = 0;         /* Page 0                   */
    retValue = 0;         /* Start clean              */

    /* Mandatory kernel initialization */

    retValue = gxSetDisplay(dispMode);
    if(retValue < 0)
    {
        PrintError("gxSetDisplay", retValue);
        return;
    }

    /* Let's set up our desired video mode */

    retValue = gxSetMode(gxGRAPHICS);
    if(retValue < 0)
    {
        PrintError("gxSetMode", retValue);
        return;
    }
```

```
/*
   The fill style and color must be set
   before doing a grDrawRect
*/

retValue = grSetFillStyle(grFHATCH, grRED,
                          grOPAQUE);
if(retValue < 0)
{
    PrintError("grSetFillStyle", retValue);
    return;
}

/*
   Set the viewport coordinates to be at
   the lower-right quadrant of screen
*/

retValue = grSetViewPort(320,240, 639,479);
if(retValue < 0)
{
    PrintError("grSetViewPort", retValue);
    return;
}

/*
   Draw a rectangle (which will be a
   hatch pattern in red) at viewport
   coordinates 0,0
*/

retValue = grDrawRect(0,0, 50,50, grFILL);
if(retValue < 0)
{
    PrintError("grDrawRect", retValue);
    return;
}

/* Wait for a user keypress, then clean up and exit */

getch();

retValue = gxSetMode(gxTEXT);
```

```
    if(retValue < 0)
    {
        PrintError("gxSetMode", retValue);
        return;
    }

    return;
}
```

grStopMouse

This function uninitializes the mouse driver.

Syntax: `int far pascal grStopMouse(void)`

Parameter: None.

Comments: You must call this function *before* exiting your program, or your system may crash! This function hides the mouse cursor and removes the mouse handler installed by `grInitMouse`. You do not need to call this function if you do not use the mouse in your application.

Return value: Success returns `gxSUCCESS`. Failure returns an error code (negative value).

See also: `grDisplayMouse`, `grTrackMouse`, `grInitMouse`

Example:

```
/*----------------------------------------------------------

Filename: grSM.C

Function: grStopMouse

Description: Finds and initializes the mouse driver,
            then stops the mouse driver. This function
            does little else. See grDisplayMouse to see
            more stuff.

Prerequisite Function(s): gxSetDisplay
                          gxSetMode
                          grInitMouse
```

```
See PrintError() function described in Appendix A

------------------------------------------------------*/

#include <stdio.h>
#include <stdlib.h>
#include <conio.h>

#include <gxlib.h>
#include <grlib.h>

void PrintError(char * funcName, int retCode);

void
main()
{
    int retValue;        /* Return value storage     */
    int dispMode;        /* 640x480x16 color         */

    /* Local initialization section */

    dispMode = gxVGA_12;  /* Set up 640x480x16 colors */
    retValue = 0;         /* Start clean               */

    /* Mandatory kernel initialization */

    retValue = gxSetDisplay(dispMode);
    if(retValue < 0)
    {
        PrintError("gxSetDisplay", retValue);
        return;
    }

    /* Let's set up our desired video mode */

    retValue = gxSetMode(gxGRAPHICS);
    if(retValue < 0)
    {
        PrintError("gxSetMode", retValue);
        return;
    }

    /* Initialize and install mouse driver */

    retValue = grInitMouse();
    if(retValue < 0)
```

```
{
    PrintError("grInitMouse", retValue);
    return;
}

/* Wait for a user keypress */

printf("Mouse initialized, but not displayed.\n");

getch();

printf("Mouse stopped.\n");

getch();

/* De-init and remove mouse driver */

retValue = grStopMouse();
if(retValue < 0)
{
    PrintError("grStopMouse", retValue);
    return;
}

/* Return to text mode */

retValue = gxSetMode(gxTEXT);
if(retValue < 0)
{
    PrintError("gxSetMode", retValue);
    return;
}

    return;
}
```

GRTRACKMOUSE

This function enables and disables automatic mouse tracking.

Syntax: `int far pascal grTrackMouse(tFlag)`

Parameter: `tFlag`

Type: `int`

Description: Mouse track flag.

Comments: This function enables or disables the automatic mouse-tracking feature. This feature moves the graphic mouse cursor whenever the user moves the physical mouse. The default setting for this feature is off, so call it at the beginning of your program if you want the mouse to move without having to track it yourself. Call this function with the argument constant grTRACK to turn tracking on and grNOTRACK to turn tracking off.

Return value: Success returns gxSUCCESS. Failure returns an error code (negative value).

See also: grInitMouse, grSetMousePos

Example:

```
/*------------------------------------------------------------

Filename: grTM.C

Function: grTrackMouse

Description: Displays the mouse; then turns it off after
            a keypress

Prerequisite Function(s): gxSetDisplay
                          gxSetMode
                          grInitMouse
                          grDisplayMouse
                          grStopMouse

See PrintError() function described in Appendix A

------------------------------------------------------------*/

#include <stdio.h>
#include <stdlib.h>
#include <conio.h>

#include <gxlib.h>
#include <grlib.h>

void PrintError(char * funcName, int retCode);
```

```
void
main()
{
    int retValue;          /* Return value storage   */
    int dispMode;          /* 640x480x16 color       */

    /* Local initialization section */

    dispMode = gxVGA_12;   /* Set up 640x480x16 colors */
    retValue = 0;          /* Start clean              */

    /* Mandatory kernel initialization */

    retValue = gxSetDisplay(dispMode);
    if(retValue < 0)
    {
        PrintError("gxSetDisplay", retValue);
        return;
    }

    /* Let's set up our desired video mode */

    retValue = gxSetMode(gxGRAPHICS);
    if(retValue < 0)
    {
        PrintError("gxSetMode", retValue);
        return;
    }

    /* Initialize and install mouse driver */

    retValue = grInitMouse();
    if(retValue < 0)
    {
        PrintError("grInitMouse", retValue);
        return;
    }

    /* Turn the mouse on */

    retValue = grDisplayMouse(grSHOW);
    if(retValue < 0)
    {
        PrintError("grDisplayMouse", retValue);
        return;
    }
```

```
printf("Press a key to track mouse movement ... ");

getch();

/* Track the mouse movement */

retValue = grTrackMouse(grTRACK);
if(retValue < 0)
{
    PrintError("grTrackMouse", retValue);
    return;
}

/* Wait for a user keypress */

printf("tracking.\nPress a key to quit.\n");

getch();

/* Turn the mouse off */

retValue = grDisplayMouse(grHIDE);
if(retValue < 0)
{
    PrintError("grDisplayMouse", retValue);
    return;
}

/* De-init and remove mouse driver */

retValue = grStopMouse();
if(retValue < 0)
{
    PrintError("grStopMouse", retValue);
    return;
}

/* Return to text mode */

retValue = gxSetMode(gxTEXT);
if(retValue < 0)
{
    PrintError("gxSetMode", retValue);
    return;
}

    return;
}
```

INTRODUCTION TO GRAPHICS EFFECTS FUNCTIONS

This chapter describes the PowerPack Graphics Effects Routines and the basic functions required for graphics programming. Several functions in this chapter reference predefined structures and data types found in the header file FXLIB.H and shown in Appendix A. To access the functions in this chapter, add the FXLIB.H file to each source file that calls these routines and add the FX_CL.LIB file (for large memory model) to your link list. Also included in this chapter are sound generation routines that add custom sound effects and even songs into your graphics programs. The sound generation routines follow a format called the Music Definition Language shown in Appendix A.

All examples in this chapter are complete, executable functions compiled in the small memory model. The one piece of source code missing from the examples is the `PrintError` function shown in Appendix A. Functions that rely on other functions to operate have been noted in the text. Each example displays the function described in bold type.

FXGETDELAY

This function returns the current effect/animation delay in milliseconds.

Syntax: `long far pascal fxGetDelay(void)`

Parameters: None.

Comments: The value returned is a long. The current delay is valid for both animation and effects. To change the current delay, call the function `fxSetDelay`.

Return value: The delay value in milliseconds (1/1000ths of a second).

See also: `fxSetDelay`

Example:

```
/*-----------------------------------------------------

Filename: fxGD.C

Function: fxGetDelay

Description: Gets the current effect delay

Prerequisite Function(s): gxSetDisplay

See PrintError() function described in Appendix A

------------------------------------------------------*/

#include <stdio.h>
#include <stdlib.h>
#include <conio.h>
```

```
#include <gxlib.h>
#include <fxlib.h>

void PrintError(char * funcName, int retCode);

void
main()
{
    int retValue;        /* Return value storage     */
    int dispMode;        /* 640x350x16 color         */
    long delay;          /* effect delay storage     */

    /* Local initialization section */

    dispMode = gxEGA_10;  /* Set up 640x350x16 colors */
    retValue = 0;         /* Start clean               */

    /* Mandatory kernel initialization */

    retValue = gxSetDisplay(dispMode);
    if(retValue < 0)
    {
        PrintError("gxSetDisplay", retValue);
        return;
    }

    /* Get the current effects delay amount */

    delay = fxGetDelay();

    /* Print the effect delay */

    printf("Current Effect Delay is %d milliseconds\n",
            delay);

    return;
}
```

fxGetEffect

This function returns the current effect type.

Syntax: `int far pascal fxGetEffect(void)`

Parameters: None.

Comments: This function returns the effect type used by fxVirtualDisplay. Refer to fxSetEffect for a listing of valid effect types and Appendix A for their definitions.

Return value: The current effect type.

See also: fxSetEffect, fxVirtualDisplay

Example:

```
/*---------------------------------------------------------

Filename: fxGE.C

Function: fxGetEffect

Description: Gets the current effect type

Prerequisite Function(s): gxSetDisplay

See PrintError() function described in Appendix A

---------------------------------------------------------*/

#include <stdio.h>
#include <stdlib.h>
#include <conio.h>

#include <gxlib.h>
#include <fxlib.h>

void PrintError(char * funcName, int retCode);

void
main()
{
    int retValue;          /* Return value storage    */
    int dispMode;          /* 640x350x16 color        */
    int effect;            /* effect type storage     */

    /* Local initialization section */

    dispMode = gxEGA_10;   /* Set up 640x350x16 colors */
    retValue = 0;          /* Start clean               */

    /* Mandatory kernel initialization */
```

```
retValue = gxSetDisplay(dispMode);
if(retValue < 0)
{
    PrintError("gxSetDisplay", retValue);
    return;
}

/* Get the current effect type */

effect = fxGetEffect();

/* Print the effect type */

printf("Current Effect Type is %d\n", effect);

return;
}
```

FxGetGrain

This function returns the transition granularity of the current effect.

Syntax: int far pascal fxGetGrain(hGrain, vGrain, subgrain)

Parameters: hGrain

Type: int *

Description: Location to store horizontal grain.

Parameters: vGrain

Type: int *

Description: Location to store vertical grain.

Parameters: subgrain

Type: int *

Description: Location to store subgrain.

Comments: The grains are the smallest increments used to display an image. For example, a grain of 8 with the fxSLIDE effect type means that the image is moved 8 pixels each time before each delay. The grain value ranges from 1 to 1,024 pixels and can be rectangular (hGrain does not have to equal vGrain). The subgrain value is used only by fxBLIND to control the speed of the blind.

Return value: Success returns gxSUCCESS. Failure returns an error code (negative value).

See also: fxSetGrain

Example:

```
/*------------------------------------------------------

Filename: fxGG.C

Function: fxGetGrain

Description: Gets the current effect granularity

Prerequisite Function(s): gxSetDisplay

See PrintError() function described in Appendix A

------------------------------------------------------*/

#include <stdio.h>
#include <stdlib.h>
#include <conio.h>

#include <gxlib.h>
#include <fxlib.h>

void PrintError(char * funcName, int retCode);

void
main()
{
    int retValue;        /* Return value storage    */
    int dispMode;        /* 640x350x16 color        */
    int hGrain;          /* horizontal grain        */
    int vGrain;          /* vertical grain          */
    int subgrain;        /* subgrain (for fxBLIND)  */
```

```
/* Local initialization section */

dispMode = gxEGA_10;   /* Set up 640x350x16 colors */
retValue = 0;          /* Start clean             */

/* Mandatory kernel initialization */

retValue = gxSetDisplay(dispMode);
if(retValue < 0)
{
    PrintError("gxSetDisplay", retValue);
    return;
}

/* Get the current grains */

retValue = fxGetGrain(&hGrain, &vGrain, &subgrain);
if(retValue < 0)
{
    PrintError("fxGetGrain", retValue);
    return;
}

/* Print the grains */

printf("Current Horizontal Grain is %d\n", hGrain);
printf("Current Vertical   Grain is %d\n", vGrain);
printf("Current Sub        Grain is %d\n",
        subgrain);

return;
}
```

FXINSTALLSOUND

This function installs the sound driver so fxPlaySong can play songs.

Syntax: int far pascal fxInstallSound(device)

Parameter: device

Type: int

Description: Must be fxPCSPEAKER.

Comments: For the PowerPack, the device argument must be set to `fxPCSPEAKER`. Refer to `fxPlaySong` to play songs after the driver is installed.

Return value: Success returns `gxSUCCESS`. Failure returns an error code (negative value).

See also: `fxPlaySong`, `fxRemoveSound`

Example:

```
/*---------------------------------------------------------

Filename: fxIS.C

Function: fxInstallSound

Description: Installs the sound driver for the speaker,
            and plays "Mary Had a Little Lamb".

Prerequisite Function(s): gxSetDisplay
                          fxInstallSound
                          fxRemoveSound
                          fxPlaySong

See PrintError() function described in Appendix A

-----------------------------------------------------*/

#include <stdio.h>
#include <stdlib.h>
#include <conio.h>

#include <gxlib.h>
#include <fxlib.h>

void PrintError(char * funcName, int retCode);

/* Global variables here... */

char playStr[] = "T240 O3 L8 EDCDEEE1 DDD1 EGG1 EDCDEEEE
                  DDEDC1";

void
```

```
main()
{
    int retValue;          /* Return value storage    */
    int dispMode;          /* 640x350x16 color        */

    /* Local initialization section */

    dispMode = gxEGA_10;   /* Set up 640x350x16 colors */
    retValue = 0;          /* Start clean              */

    /* Mandatory kernel initialization */

    retValue = gxSetDisplay(dispMode);
    if(retValue < 0)
    {
        PrintError("gxSetDisplay", retValue);
        return;
    }

    /* Must install the sound driver first */

    retValue = fxInstallSound(fxPCSPEAKER);
    if(retValue < 0)
    {
        PrintError("fxInstallSound", retValue);
        return;
    }

    /* Start the song */

    printf("Playing 'Mary Had a Little Lamb' ...");

    retValue = fxPlaySong(playStr, 1);
    if(retValue < 0)
    {
        PrintError("fxPlaySong", retValue);
        return;
    }

    printf(" Done.\n");

    /* Remove the sound driver */
```

```
    retValue = fxRemoveSound(fxPCSPEAKER);
    if(retValue < 0)
    {
        PrintError("fxRemoveSound", retValue);
        return;
    }

    return;
}
```

FXKILLSOUND

This function stops the sound that's being played.

Syntax: `int far pascal fxKillSound(feature)`

Parameter: `feature`

Type: `int`

Description: Must be `fxSNG`.

Comments: For the PowerPack, the feature argument must be set to `fxSNG`. Refer to `fxPlaySong` or `fxPlayTone`, respectively, to start a song or tone.

Return value: Success returns `gxSUCCESS`. Failure returns an error code (negative value).

See also: `fxPlaySound`, `fxPlaySong`

Example:

```
/*-----------------------------------------------------------

Filename: fxKS.C

Function: fxKillSound

Description: Plays "Mary Had a Little Lamb" twice. If
            the user presses a key beforehand, the
            song stops.

Prerequisite Function(s): gxSetDisplay
                          fxInstallSound
```

```
                        fxRemoveSound
                        fxPlaySong

See PrintError() function described in Appendix A

------------------------------------------------------*/

#include <stdio.h>
#include <stdlib.h>
#include <conio.h>

#include <gxlib.h>
#include <fxlib.h>

void PrintError(char * funcName, int retCode);

/* Global variables here... */

char playStr[] = "MB T120 O3 L8 EDCDEEE1 DDD1 EGG1
EDCDEEEE DDEDC1";

void
main()
{
    int retValue;          /* Return value storage    */
    int dispMode;          /* 640x350x16 color        */

    /* Local initialization section */

    dispMode = gxEGA_10;   /* Set up 640x350x16 colors */
    retValue = 0;          /* Start clean              */

    /* Mandatory kernel initialization */

    retValue = gxSetDisplay(dispMode);
    if(retValue < 0)
    {
        PrintError("gxSetDisplay", retValue);
        return;
    }

    /* Must install the sound driver first */

    retValue = fxInstallSound(fxPCSPEAKER);
    if(retValue < 0)
```

```
    {
        PrintError("fxInstallSound", retValue);
        return;
    }

    /* Start the song */

    printf("Playing 'Mary Had a Little Lamb' ...");

    retValue = fxPlaySong(playStr, 2);
    if(retValue < 0)
    {
        PrintError("fxPlaySong", retValue);
        return;
    }

    printf("in the background.\n\nPress any key to kill ...");

    getch();

    retValue = fxKillSound(fxSNG);
    if(retValue < 0)
    {
        PrintError("fxPlaySong", retValue);
        return;
    }

    printf(" killed.\n");

    /* Remove the sound driver */

    retValue = fxRemoveSound(fxPCSPEAKER);
    if(retValue < 0)
    {
        PrintError("fxRemoveSound", retValue);
        return;
    }

    return;
}
```

FXPLAYSONG

This function plays the specified string of notes, and plays it again, if requested.

Syntax: `int far pascal fxPlaySong(playStr, loopNum)`

Parameter: `playStr`

Type: `char *`

Description: Pointer to string containing Music Definition commands.

Parameter: `loopNum`

Type: `int`

Description: Number of loops desired (times to play).

Comments: The format of the string must correspond to the Music Definition Language described in Appendix A. The music can be played in the foreground or background. Before the `fxPlaySong` function will work, you must install the sound driver first by calling `fxInstallSound`. Also, you must call `fxRemoveSound` to remove the sound driver or a machine lockup occurs. The argument `loopNum` (ranging from 1 to 65,535 or the value `fxINFINITE`) represents the number of times you want the song buffer played.

Return value: Success returns `gxSUCCESS`. Failure returns an error code (negative value).

See also: `fxInstallSound`, `fxRemoveSound`, `fxPlayTone`

Example:

```
/*------------------------------------------------------

Filename: fxPS.C

Function: fxPlaySong

Description: Plays "Mary Had a Little Lamb"

Prerequisite Function(s): gxSetDisplay
                          fxInstallSound
                          fxRemoveSound
```

```
See PrintError() function described in Appendix A

-------------------------------------------------------*/

#include <stdio.h>
#include <stdlib.h>
#include <conio.h>

#include <gxlib.h>
#include <fxlib.h>

void PrintError(char * funcName, int retCode);

/* Global variables here... */

char playStr[] = "T120 O3 L8 EDCDEEE1 DDD1 EGG1 EDCDEEEE
                  DDEDC1";

void
main()
{
    int retValue;         /* Return value storage     */
    int dispMode;         /* 640x350x16 color         */

    /* Local initialization section */

    dispMode = gxEGA_10;  /* Set up 640x350x16 colors */
    retValue = 0;         /* Start clean               */

    /* Mandatory kernel initialization */

    retValue = gxSetDisplay(dispMode);
    if(retValue < 0)
    {
        PrintError("gxSetDisplay", retValue);
        return;
    }

    /* Must install the sound driver first */

    retValue = fxInstallSound(fxPCSPEAKER);
    if(retValue < 0)
    {
        PrintError("fxInstallSound", retValue);
        return;
    }
```

```
/* Start the song */

printf("Playing 'Mary Had a Little Lamb' ...");

retValue = fxPlaySong(playStr, 1);
if(retValue < 0)
{
    PrintError("fxPlaySong", retValue);
    return;
}

printf(" Done.\n");

/* Remove the sound driver */

retValue = fxRemoveSound(fxPCSPEAKER);
if(retValue < 0)
{
    PrintError("fxRemoveSound", retValue);
    return;
}

return;
}
```

FXPLAYTONE

This function plays the specified tone on the PC speaker.

Syntax: `int far pascal fxPlayTone(device, freq, duration)`

Parameter: `device`

Type: `int`

Description: Must be `fxPCSPEAKER`.

Parameter: `freq`

Type: `int`

Description: Tone frequency in hertz.

Parameter: duration

Type: long

Description: Duration of tone in milliseconds.

Comments: For the PowerPack, this function plays only on the PC speaker. Therefore, the first argument device must be set to fxPCSPEAKER.

Return value: Success returns gxSUCCESS. Failure returns an error code (negative value).

See also: fxPlaySong

Example:

```
/*-------------------------------------------------------------

Filename: fxPT.C

Function: fxPlayTone

Description: Plays 400 hertz tone for 5 seconds.

Prerequisite Function(s): gxSetDisplay

See PrintError() function described in Appendix A

-----------------------------------------------------------*/
#include <stdio.h>
#include <stdlib.h>
#include <conio.h>

#include <gxlib.h>
#include <fxlib.h>

void PrintError(char * funcName, int retCode);

void
main()
{
    int retValue;       /* Return value storage     */
    int dispMode;       /* 640x350x16 color         */
```

```
/* Local initialization section */

dispMode = gxEGA_10;   /* Set up 640x350x16 colors */
retValue = 0;          /* Start clean            */

/* Mandatory kernel initialization */

retValue = gxSetDisplay(dispMode);
if(retValue < 0)
{
    PrintError("gxSetDisplay", retValue);
    return;
}

/* Start the tone */

printf("Playing 400 hertz tone for 5 seconds ...");

retValue = fxPlayTone(fxPCSPEAKER, 400, 5000);
if(retValue < 0)
{
    PrintError("fxPlayTone", retValue);
    return;
}

printf(" Done.\n");

return;
}
```

fxRemoveSound

This function removes the sound driver installed by
fxInstallSound.

Syntax: int far pascal fxRemoveSound(device)

Parameter: device

Type: int

Description: Must be fxPCSPEAKER.

Comments: For the PowerPack, the device argument must be set
to fxPCSPEAKER. This function must be called before exiting your
application or a lockup is likely to occur.

Return value: Success returns gxSUCCESS. Failure returns an error code (negative value).

See also: fxPlaySong, fxInstallSound

Example:

```
/*-----------------------------------------------------------

Filename: fxRS.C

Function: fxRemoveSound

Description: Installs the sound driver for the speaker,
             plays "Mary Had a Little Lamb," and removes
             the sound driver

Prerequisite Function(s): gxSetDisplay
                          fxInstallSound
                          fxPlaySong

See PrintError() function described in Appendix A

-----------------------------------------------------------*/

#include <stdio.h>
#include <stdlib.h>
#include <conio.h>

#include <gxlib.h>
#include <fxlib.h>

void PrintError(char * funcName, int retCode);

/* Global variables here... */

char playStr[] = "T180 O3 L8 EDCDEEE1 DDD1 EGG1 EDCDEEEE
                  DDEDC1";

void
main()
{
    int retValue;       /* Return value storage    */
    int dispMode;       /* 640x350x16 color        */

    /* Local initialization section */
```

```
dispMode = gxEGA_10;    /* Set up 640x350x16 colors */
retValue = 0;           /* Start clean              */

/* Mandatory kernel initialization */

retValue = gxSetDisplay(dispMode);
if(retValue < 0)
{
    PrintError("gxSetDisplay", retValue);
    return;
}

/* Must install the sound driver first */

retValue = fxInstallSound(fxPCSPEAKER);
if(retValue < 0)
{
    PrintError("fxInstallSound", retValue);
    return;
}

/* Start the song */

printf("Playing 'Mary Had a Little Lamb' ...");

retValue = fxPlaySong(playStr, 1);
if(retValue < 0)
{
    PrintError("fxPlaySong", retValue);
    return;
}

printf(" Done.\n");

/* Remove the sound driver */

retValue = fxRemoveSound(fxPCSPEAKER);
if(retValue < 0)
{
    PrintError("fxRemoveSound", retValue);
    return;
}

return;
}
```

FXSETDELAY

This function changes the current effect/animation delay to the specified delay value.

Syntax: `int far pascal fxSetDelay(delay)`

Parameter: `delay`

Type: `long`

Description: New delay in milliseconds.

Comments: The new delay takes effect for all transitions and animations after the call to this function is complete. The delay occurs between each effect grain or animated motion. Therefore, the image size, grain size, time delay, and current display mode all affect the overall speed of the animation or transition.

Return value: Success returns `gxSUCCESS`. Failure returns an error code (negative value).

See also: `fxGetDelay`

Example:

```
/*----------------------------------------------------------

Filename: fxSD.C

Function: fxSetDelay

Description: Sets the current effect delay to 50
            milliseconds

Prerequisite Function(s): gxSetDisplay
                          fxGetDelay

See PrintError() function described in Appendix A

----------------------------------------------------------*/

#include <stdio.h>
#include <stdlib.h>
#include <conio.h>
```

```
#include <gxlib.h>
#include <fxlib.h>

void PrintError(char * funcName, int retCode);

void
main()
{
    int retValue;         /* Return value storage    */
    int dispMode;         /* 640x350x16 color        */
    long delay;           /* effect delay storage    */
    long newDelay;        /* delay to set            */

    /* Local initialization section */

    dispMode = gxEGA_10;  /* Set up 640x350x16 colors */
    retValue = 0;         /* Start clean              */

    /* Mandatory kernel initialization */

    retValue = gxSetDisplay(dispMode);
    if(retValue < 0)
    {
        PrintError("gxSetDisplay", retValue);
        return;
    }

    newDelay = 50;    /* 50 millisecond delay */

    retValue = fxSetDelay(newDelay);
    if(retValue < 0)
    {
        PrintError("fxSetDelay", retValue);
        return;
    }

    /* Get the current effects delay amount */

    delay = fxGetDelay();

    /* Print the effect delay */

    printf("Current Effect Delay is %d milliseconds\n",
            delay);

    return;
}
```

FXSETEFFECT

This function changes the current effect type to the specified value.

Syntax: `int far pascal fxSetEffect(effect)`

Parameter: `effect`

Type: `int`

Description: New effect type.

Comments: The following list contains the valid effect types.

Effect Type	Description
`fxBLIND`	Venetian blinds wipe
`fxCRUSH`	Crush wipe from middle
`fxDIAGONAL`	Diagonal wipe
`fxDRIP`	Drip-smear wipe
`fxEXPLODE`	Exploding parts wipe
`fxRANDOM`	Random parts wipe
`fxSAND`	Similar to `fxDRIP`
`fxSLIDE`	Slide image wipe
`fxSPIRAL`	Circular wipe
`fxSPLIT`	Opposite of `fxCRUSH`
`fxWEAVE`	Similar to `fxBLIND`
`fxWIPE`	Straight wipe from side to side

Return value: Success returns `gxSUCCESS`. Failure returns an error code (negative value).

See also: `fxGetEffect`

Example:

```
/*--------------------------------------------------------

Filename: fxSE.C

Function: fxSetEffect
```

```
Description: Sets the current effect type to EXPLODE
             (4), then gets the effect and prints the
             value.

Prerequisite Function(s): gxSetDisplay
                          fxGetEffect

See PrintError() function described in Appendix A

------------------------------------------------------*/

#include <stdio.h>
#include <stdlib.h>
#include <conio.h>

#include <gxlib.h>
#include <fxlib.h>

void PrintError(char * funcName, int retCode);

void
main()
{
    int retValue;        /* Return value storage   */
    int dispMode;        /* 640x350x16 color       */
    int effect;          /* effect type storage    */

    /* Local initialization section */

    dispMode = gxEGA_10;  /* Set up 640x350x16 colors */
    retValue = 0;         /* Start clean               */

    /* Mandatory kernel initialization */

    retValue = gxSetDisplay(dispMode);
    if(retValue < 0)
    {
        PrintError("gxSetDisplay", retValue);
        return;
    }

    /* Set the effect to fxEXPLODE */
```

```
    retValue = fxSetEffect(fxEXPLODE);
    if(retValue < 0)
    {
        PrintError("fxSetEffect", retValue);
        return;
    }

    /* Get the current effect type */

    effect = fxGetEffect();

    /* Print the effect type */

    printf("Current Effect Type is %d\n", effect);

    return;
}
```

FXSETFREQUENCY

This function sets the current frequency of the PC speaker to a specified frequency.

Syntax: `int far pascal fxSetFrequency(freq)`

Parameter: `freq`

Type: `int`

Description: Tone frequency in hertz.

Comments: This function enables you to preset the frequency of the PC speaker before you turn on the speaker with a call to `fxSetSpeaker`. This directly controls the sound instead of using the `fxPlayTone` or `fxPlaySong` functions.

Return value: Success returns `gxSUCCESS`. Failure returns an error code (negative value).

See also: `fxSetSpeaker`, `fxPlayTone`, `fxPlaySong`

Example:

```
/*--------------------------------------------------------

Filename: fxSF.C
```

```
Function: fxSetFrequency

Description: Turns on the speaker and waits for a
             keypress, then sets the speaker for 2000
             hertz, and waits for a keypress

Prerequisite Function(s): gxSetDisplay
                          fxSetSpeaker

See PrintError() function described in Appendix A

-------------------------------------------------------*/

#include <stdio.h>
#include <stdlib.h>
#include <conio.h>

#include <gxlib.h>
#include <fxlib.h>

void PrintError(char * funcName, int retCode);

void
main()
{
    int retValue;       /* Return value storage    */
    int dispMode;       /* 640x350x16 color        */

    /* Local initialization section */

    dispMode = gxEGA_10;  /* Set up 640x350x16 colors */
    retValue = 0;         /* Start clean              */

    /* Mandatory kernel initialization */

    retValue = gxSetDisplay(dispMode);
    if(retValue < 0)
    {
        PrintError("gxSetDisplay", retValue);
        return;
    }

    /*
       First, we turn the speaker on at its
       default frequency
    */
```

```
retValue = fxSetSpeaker(fxPCSPEAKER, fxON);
if(retValue < 0)
{
    PrintError("fxSetSpeaker", retValue);
    return;
}

printf("The speaker is ON at default
        frequency\n\n");
printf("Press any key to change to 2000 Hz ...");

/* Get a keypress */
getch();

/* Set the new frequency */

retValue = fxSetFrequency(2000);
if(retValue < 0)
{
    PrintError("fxSetFrequency", retValue);
    return;
}

printf(" Done.\n\n");
printf("Press any key to turn speaker off ...");

/* Get a keypress */
getch();

/* Turn the speaker off */

retValue = fxSetSpeaker(fxPCSPEAKER, fxOFF);
if(retValue < 0)
{
    PrintError("fxSetSpeaker", retValue);
    return;
}

printf(" Done.\n");

/* Restore the default frequency (not required) */

retValue = fxSetFrequency(900);
if(retValue < 0)
```

```
    {
        PrintError("fxSetFrequency", retValue);
        return;
    }

    return;
}
```

fxSetGrain

This function sets the transition granularity of the current effect type.

Syntax: `int far pascal fxSetGrain(hGrain, vGrain, subgrain)`

Parameter: `hGrain`

Type: `int`

Description: New horizontal grain.

Parameter: `vGrain`

Type: `int`

Description: New vertical grain.

Parameter: `subgrain`

Type: `int`

Description: New subgrain.

Comments: The grains are the smallest increments used to display an image. For example, a grain of 16 with the `fxDIAGONAL` effect type means that the image is displayed diagonally in boxes 16-pixels square. The grain value ranges from 1 to 1,024 pixels and can be rectangular (`hGrain` does not have to equal `vGrain`). The `subgrain` value is used only by `fxBLIND` to control the speed of the blind.

Return value: Success returns gxSUCCESS. Failure returns an error code (negative value).

See also: fxGetEffect

Example:

```
/*-------------------------------------------------------

Filename: fxSG.C

Function: fxSetGrain

Description: Sets the current effect granularity to 16
            horizontal, and 16 vertical

Prerequisite Function(s): gxSetDisplay
                          fxGetGrain

See PrintError() function described in Appendix A

-------------------------------------------------------*/

#include <stdio.h>
#include <stdlib.h>
#include <conio.h>

#include <gxlib.h>
#include <fxlib.h>

void PrintError(char * funcName, int retCode);

void
main()
{
    int retValue;       /* Return value storage      */
    int dispMode;       /* 640x350x16 color          */
    int hGrain;         /* horizontal grain          */
    int vGrain;         /* vertical grain            */
    int subgrain;       /* subgrain (for fxBLIND)    */

    /* Local initialization section */

    dispMode = gxEGA_10;  /* Set up 640x350x16 colors */
    retValue = 0;         /* Start clean               */
```

```
/* Mandatory kernel initialization */

retValue = gxSetDisplay(dispMode);
if(retValue < 0)
{
    PrintError("gxSetDisplay", retValue);
    return;
}

/* Set the new grains */

retValue = fxSetGrain(16, 16, 2);
if(retValue < 0)
{
    PrintError("fxSetGrain", retValue);
    return;
}

/* Get the current grains */

retValue = fxGetGrain(&hGrain, &vGrain, &subgrain);
if(retValue < 0)
{
    PrintError("fxGetGrain", retValue);
    return;
}

/* Print the grains */

printf("Current Horizontal Grain is %d\n", hGrain);
printf("Current Vertical  Grain is %d\n", vGrain);
printf("Current Sub       Grain is %d\n",
        subgrain);

return;
}
```

FXSETSPEAKER

This function turns the PC speaker on or off.

Syntax: `int far pascal fxSetSpeaker(device, sFlag)`

Parameter: `device`

Type: int

Description: Must be fxPCSPEAKER.

Parameter: sFlag

Type: int

Description: Either fxON or fxOFF.

Comments: This function turns the PC speaker on or off as specified by the argument sFlag. Setting sFlag to fxON turns on the speaker; setting it to fxOFF turns off the speaker. For the PowerPack, the argument device must be set to fxPCSPEAKER.

Return value: Success returns gxSUCCESS. Failure returns an error code (negative value).

See also: fxSetFrequency, fxPlayTone, fxPlaySong

Example:

```
/*----------------------------------------------------------

Filename: fxSS.C

Function: fxSetSpeaker

Description: Turns on the speaker, waits for a keypress,
            then turns it off

Prerequisite Function(s): gxSetDisplay

See PrintError() function described in Appendix A

----------------------------------------------------------*/

#include <stdio.h>
#include <stdlib.h>
#include <conio.h>

#include <gxlib.h>
#include <fxlib.h>
```

```
void PrintError(char * funcName, int retCode);

void
main()
{
    int retValue;           /* Return value storage    */
    int dispMode;           /* 640x350x16 color        */

    /* Local initialization section */

    dispMode = gxEGA_10;    /* Set up 640x350x16 colors */
    retValue = 0;           /* Start clean              */

    /* Mandatory kernel initialization */

    retValue = gxSetDisplay(dispMode);
    if(retValue < 0)
    {
        PrintError("gxSetDisplay", retValue);
        return;
    }

    /* Turn the speaker on */

    retValue = fxSetSpeaker(fxPCSPEAKER, fxON);
    if(retValue < 0)
    {
        PrintError("fxSetSpeaker", retValue);
        return;
    }

    printf("The speaker is ON at default
            frequency\n\n");
    printf("Press any key to turn speaker off ...");

    /* Get a keypress */
    getch();

    /* Turn the speaker off */

    retValue = fxSetSpeaker(fxPCSPEAKER, fxOFF);
    if(retValue < 0)
    {
        PrintError("fxSetSpeaker", retValue);
        return;
    }
```

```
    printf(" Done.\n");

    return;
}
```

FXSOUNDLEFT

This function returns the amount of sound data left to play.

Syntax: `long far pascal fxSoundLeft(feature)`

Parameter: `feature`

Type: `int`

Description: Must be `fxSNG`.

Comments: For the PowerPack, this function returns the number of notes left to be played.

Return value: Success returns number of notes remaining. Failure returns an error code (negative value).

See also: `fxPlaySong`

Example:

```
/*-----------------------------------------------------

Filename: fxSL.C

Function: fxSoundLeft

Description: Plays "Mary Had a Little Lamb," then prints
            the number of remaining notes as the song
            plays.

Prerequisite Function(s): gxSetDisplay
                          fxInstallSound
                          fxRemoveSound
                          fxPlaySong

See PrintError() function described in Appendix A

-----------------------------------------------------*/
```

```c
#include <stdio.h>
#include <stdlib.h>
#include <conio.h>

#include <gxlib.h>
#include <fxlib.h>

void PrintError(char * funcName, int retCode);

/* Global variables here... */

char playStr[] = "MB T120 L8 O3 EDCDEEE1 DDD1 EGG1
                EDCDEEEE DDEDC1";

void
main()
{
    int retValue;          /* Return value storage    */
    int dispMode;          /* 640x350x16 color        */
    long notesLeft;        /* The number of notes left */

    /* Local initialization section */

    dispMode = gxEGA_10;   /* Set up 640x350x16 colors */
    retValue = 0;          /* Start clean              */

    /* Mandatory kernel initialization */

    retValue = gxSetDisplay(dispMode);
    if(retValue < 0)
    {
        PrintError("gxSetDisplay", retValue);
        return;
    }

    /* Must install the sound driver first */

    retValue = fxInstallSound(fxPCSPEAKER);
    if(retValue < 0)
    {
        PrintError("fxInstallSound", retValue);
        return;
    }
```

```
/* Start the song */

printf("Playing 'Mary Had a Little Lamb' ...\n\n");

retValue = fxPlaySong(playStr, 1);
if(retValue < 0)
{
    PrintError("fxPlaySong", retValue);
    return;
}

/* Print the number of remaining notes */

while( (notesLeft = fxSoundLeft(fxSNG)) > 0){
    printf("There are %d notes left\n", notesLeft);
}

printf(" Done.\n");

/* Remove the sound driver */

retValue = fxRemoveSound(fxPCSPEAKER);
if(retValue < 0)
{
    PrintError("fxRemoveSound", retValue);
    return;
}

return;
}
```

FXVIRTUALDISPLAY

This function initiates the desired effects on the specified image.

Syntax: `int far pascal fxVirtualDisplay(vhPtr, vx, vy, x1, y1, x2, y2, dir)`

Parameter: `vhPtr`

Type: GXHEADER *

Description: Location to store virtual header information.

Parameter: vx, vy

Type: int

Description: Offset into virtual image to begin displaying image.

Parameter: x1, y1

Type: int

Description: Upper-left corner of the display window.

Parameter: x2, y2

Type: int

Description: Lower-right corner of the display window.

Parameter: dir

Type: int

Description: Direction to display effect.

Comments: This function is the main function for displaying image effects. It takes a previously loaded image and performs the specified effect at the virtual location vx,vy within the virtual buffer. A window—created on the display from x1,y1 to x2,y2— defines how much of the virtual buffer is displayed. Refer to fxSetEffect to see the effect type descriptions and Appendix A for the constant definitions of the effect types. The direction dir can be set to one of the four direction options shown in the following listing.

Effect Type	Option 1	Option 2	Option 3	Option 4
fxBLIND	fxHORIZ	fxVERT	N/A	N/A
fxCRUSH	fxHORIZ	fxVERT	N/A	N/A
fxDIAGONAL	fxUP+	fxUP+	fxDOWN+	fxDOWN+
	fxRIGHT	fxLEFT	fxRIGHT	fxLEFT
fxDRIP	fxUP	fxDOWN	N/A	N/A
fxEXPLODE	fxIN	fxOUT	N/A	N/A
fxRANDOM	fxNONE	N/A	N/A	N/A
fxSAND	fxUP	fxDOWN	N/A	N/A
fxSLIDE	fxUP	fxDOWN	fxRIGHT	fxLEFT
fxSPIRAL	fxIN	fxOUT	N/A	N/A
fxSPLIT	fxHORIZ	fxVERT	N/A	N/A
fxWEAVE	fxHORIZ	fxVERT	N/A	N/A
fxWIPE	fxUP	fxDOWN	fxRIGHT	fxLEFT

Return value: Success returns gxSUCCESS. Failure returns an error code (negative value).

See also: fxSetEffect, fxSetGrain, fxSetDelay

Example:

```
/*-----------------------------------------------------------

Filename: fxVD.C

Function: fxVirtualDisplay

Description: Creates a full screen buffer, clears it
             green, and displays it in the fxWEAVE
             effect

Prerequisite Function(s): gxSetDisplay
                          gxSetMode
                          gxCreateVirtual
                          gxClearVirtual
                          gxDestroyVirtual
                          fxSetEffect
                          fxSetGrain
```

```
See PrintError() function described in Appendix A

------------------------------------------------------*/

#include <stdio.h>
#include <stdlib.h>
#include <conio.h>

#include <gxlib.h>
#include <grlib.h>
#include <fxlib.h>

void PrintError(char * funcName, int retCode);

/* Global variables here... */

GXHEADER vHeader;           /* Storage for virtual bufs */

void
main()
{
    int retValue;           /* Return value storage    */
    int dispMode;           /* 640x480x16 color        */

    /* Local initialization section */

    dispMode = gxVGA_12;  /* Set up 640x480x16 colors */
    retValue = 0;           /* Start clean             */

    /* Mandatory kernel initialization */

    retValue = gxSetDisplay(dispMode);
    if(retValue < 0)
    {
        PrintError("gxSetDisplay", retValue);
        return;
    }

    /* Let's set up our desired video mode */

    retValue = gxSetMode(gxGRAPHICS);
    if(retValue < 0)
    {
```

```
        PrintError("gxSetMode", retValue);
        return;
}

/* Set the effect to weave */

retValue = fxSetEffect(fxWEAVE);
if(retValue < 0)
{
    PrintError("fxSetEffect", retValue);
    return;
}

/* Set the grains to 16x16 */

retValue = fxSetGrain(16,16,1);
if(retValue < 0)
{
    PrintError("fxSetGrain", retValue);
    return;
}

/*
    Create the virtual buffer in conventional memory
    that is 640 by 480 in pixels
*/

retValue = gxCreateVirtual(gxCMM, &vHeader,
                           dispMode, 640, 480);
if(retValue < 0)
{
    PrintError("gxCreateVirtual", retValue);
    return;
}

/* Once created, clear it to green.  */

retValue = gxClearVirtual(&vHeader, gxGREEN);
if(retValue < 0)
{
    PrintError("gxClearVirtual", retValue);
    return;
}

/*
```

```
      Display it on the screen with the effect,
      weaving horizontally
*/
retValue = fxVirtualDisplay(&vHeader,
                0,0, 0,0, 639,479, fxHORIZ);
if(retValue < 0)
{
    PrintError("fxVirtualDisplay", retValue);
    return;
}

getch();

/* Deallocate both virtual blocks */

retValue = gxDestroyVirtual(&vHeader);
if(retValue < 0)
{
    PrintError("gxDestroyVirtual", retValue);
    return;
}

retValue = gxSetMode(gxTEXT);
if(retValue < 0)
{
    PrintError("gxSetMode", retValue);
    return;
}

    return;
}
```

INTRODUCTION TO PCX IMAGE FILE FUNCTIONS

This chapter describes PowerPack's PCX routines and the basic functions required for graphics programming. Several functions in this chapter reference predefined structures and data types found in the header file PCXLIB.H and shown in Appendix A. To access the functions in this chapter, add the PCXLIB.H file to each source file that calls these routines and add the PCX_CL.LIB file (for the large memory model) to your link list.

All examples in this chapter are complete, executable functions compiled in the small memory model. The one piece of source code missing from the examples is the PrintError function shown in Appendix A. Functions that rely on other functions to operate have been noted in the text. Each example displays the function described in bold type.

PCXFILEIMAGE

This function creates a virtual buffer and loads the specified PCX file into the buffer.

Syntax: `int far pascal pcxFileImage(vType, fileName, vhPtr, dType)`

Parameter: `vType`

Type: `int`

Description: Virtual memory type.

Parameter: `fileName`

Type: `char *`

Description: Pointer to PCX image file.

Parameter: `vhPtr`

Type: `GXHEADER *`

Description: Location to store virtual header information.

Parameter: `dType`

Type: `int`

Description: Display type.

Comments: This function checks the image to see if it is a valid PCX image. It then creates a virtual buffer, loads the image into the buffer, and returns the detected display type. You can display the image on-screen using `gxVirtualDisplay`. The argument

vType is used to determine in which type of memory the virtual
buffer is to be created (gxCMM). The argument dType can be one of
the valid display types or can be set to gxDETECT to use the current
display mode. Be sure you load a file whose pixel depth matches
the specified display mode's pixel depth. Refer to gxSetDisplay
for a listing of valid display types and pixel depths. You must call
gxFreeImage to free the virtual buffer before you can exit your
application.

Return value: Success returns image display type. Failure returns
an error code (negative value).

See also: pcxFreeImage, gxVirtualDisplay

Example:

```
/*-------------------------------------------------------

Filename: pcxFI.C

Function: pcxFileImage

Description: Loads PCX file into a virtual buffer
             created by pcxFileImage and displays it on
             the screen

Prerequisite Function(s): gxSetDisplay
                          gxSetMode
                          gxVirtualDisplay
                          pcxFreeImage

See PrintError() function described in Appendix A

-------------------------------------------------------*/

#include <stdio.h>
#include <stdlib.h>
#include <conio.h>

#include <gxlib.h>
#include <pcxlib.h>

void PrintError(char * funcName, int retCode);

/* Global variables here... */
```

```
char * pcxFile = "Genus.PCX";
GXHEADER vHeader;

void
main()
{
    int retValue;        /* Return value storage   */
    int dispMode;        /* 640x480x16 color       */

    /* Local initialization section */

    dispMode = gxVGA_12; /* Set up 640x480x16 colors */
    retValue = 0;        /* Start clean             */

    /* Mandatory kernel initialization */

    retValue = gxSetDisplay(dispMode);
    if(retValue < 0)
    {
        PrintError("gxSetDisplay", retValue);
        return;
    }

    /* Verifies, then loads image into buffer */

    retValue = pcxFileImage(gxCMM, pcxFile,
                            &vHeader, dispMode);

    if(retValue < 0)
    {
        PrintError("pcxFileImage", retValue);
        return;
    }

    /* Let's set up our desired video mode */

    retValue = gxSetMode(gxGRAPHICS);
    if(retValue < 0)
    {
        PrintError("gxSetMode", retValue);
        return;
    }

    retValue = gxVirtualDisplay(&vHeader,
                            0,0, 0,0, 639,479, 0);
    if(retValue < 0)
```

```
{
    PrintError("gxVirtualDisplay", retValue);
    return;
}

/* Wait for a user keypress */

getch();

/* Free the allocated memory before leaving */

retValue = pcxFreeImage(&vHeader);
if(retValue < 0)
{
    PrintError("pcxFreeImage", retValue);
    return;
}

/* Clean up and exit */

retValue = gxSetMode(gxTEXT);
if(retValue < 0)
{
    PrintError("gxSetMode", retValue);
    return;
}

    return;
}
```

pcxFreeImage

This function frees the memory allocated from the call to
pcxFileImage.

Syntax: int far pascal pcxFileImage(vhPtr)

Parameter: vhPtr

Type: GXHEADER *

Description: Pointer to the virtual buffer.

Comments: pcxFreeImage performs essentially the same task as gxDestroyVisual, freeing the memory created by a call to pcxFileImage.

Return value: Success returns gxSUCCESS. Failure returns an error code (negative value).

See also: pcxFileImage

Example:

```
/*---------------------------------------------------------

Filename: pcxFRI.C

Function: pcxFreeImage

Description: Loads PCX file into a virtual buffer
             created by pcxFileImage, displays it on the
             screen, and then frees the allocated memory

Prerequisite Function(s): gxSetDisplay
                          gxSetMode
                          gxVirtualDisplay
                          pcxFileImage

See PrintError() function described in Appendix A

---------------------------------------------------------*/

#include <stdio.h>
#include <stdlib.h>
#include <conio.h>

#include <gxlib.h>
#include <pcxlib.h>

void PrintError(char * funcName, int retCode);

/* Global variables here... */

char * pcxFile = "Genus.PCX";
GXHEADER vHeader;

void
main()
{
```

```
int retValue;        /* Return value storage   */
int dispMode;        /* 640x480x16 color       */

/* Local initialization section */

dispMode = gxVGA_12; /* Set up 640x480x16 colors */
retValue = 0;        /* Start clean            */

/* Mandatory kernel initialization */

retValue = gxSetDisplay(dispMode);
if(retValue < 0)
{
    PrintError("gxSetDisplay", retValue);
    return;
}

/* Verifies, then loads image into buffer */

retValue = pcxFileImage(gxCMM, pcxFile,
                        &vHeader, dispMode);

if(retValue < 0)
{
    PrintError("pcxFileImage", retValue);
    return;
}

/* Let's set up our desired video mode */

retValue = gxSetMode(gxGRAPHICS);
if(retValue < 0)
{
    PrintError("gxSetMode", retValue);
    return;
}

retValue = gxVirtualDisplay(&vHeader,
                        0,0, 0,0, 639,479, 0);
if(retValue < 0)
{
    PrintError("gxVirtualDisplay", retValue);
    return;
}

/* Wait for a user keypress */
```

```
    getch();

    /* Free the allocated memory before leaving */

    retValue = pcxFreeImage(&vHeader);
    if(retValue < 0)
    {
        PrintError("pcxFreeImage", retValue);
        return;
    }

    /* Clean up and exit */

    retValue = gxSetMode(gxTEXT);
    if(retValue < 0)
    {
        PrintError("gxSetMode", retValue);
        return;
    }

    return;
}
```

PCXGETFILEHEADER

This function returns header information about a specified PCX file.

Syntax: `int far pascal pcxGetFileHeader(fileName, header)`

Parameter: `fileName`

Type: `char *`

Description: Pointer to PCX file.

Parameter: `header`

Type: `PCXHEADER *`

Description: Location to store the PCX file header.

Comments: The function extracts the header from the PCX image file and returns it into the memory location pointed to by header. This header includes information such as image resolution and number of colors. This information helps determine the display type necessary for proper display of the image file. Refer to Appendix A for a description of the PCXHEADER structure.

Return value: Success returns gxSUCCESS. Failure returns an error code (negative value).

See also: pcxFileImage, pcxGetFilePalette, pcxGetFileType

Example:

```
/*------------------------------------------------------

Filename: pcxGFH.C

Function: pcxGetFileHeader

Description: Returns header information about GENUS.PCX

Prerequisite Function(s): gxSetDisplay
                          gxSetMode

See PrintError() function described in Appendix A

------------------------------------------------------*/

#include <stdio.h>
#include <stdlib.h>
#include <conio.h>

#include <gxlib.h>
#include <pcxlib.h>

void PrintError(char * funcName, int retCode);

/* Global variables here... */

char * pcxFile = "Genus.PCX";
PCXHEADER pcxHdr;

void
main()
{
```

```
int retValue;       /* Return value storage   */
int dispMode;       /* 640x480x16 color       */

/* Local initialization section */

dispMode = gxVGA_12; /* Set up 640x480x16 colors */
retValue = 0;        /* Start clean              */

/* Mandatory kernel initialization */

retValue = gxSetDisplay(dispMode);
if(retValue < 0)
{
    PrintError("gxSetDisplay", retValue);
    return;
}

/* Get the header information */

retValue = pcxGetFileHeader(pcxFile, &pcxHdr);
if(retValue < 0)
{
    PrintError("pcxGetFileHeader", retValue);
    return;
}

/* Print some of the information */

printf("%s Header info - Picture dimensions: 
        ",pcxFile);
printf("%d,%d %d,%d\n", pcxHdr.x1, pcxHdr.y1,
                        pcxHdr.x2, pcxHdr.y2);

return;
}
```

PCXGETFILEPALETTE

This function returns palette information about a specified PCX file.

Syntax: int far pascal pcxGetFilePalette(dType, fileName, palette)

Parameter: dType

Type: int

Description: Display type of file.

Parameter: fileName

Type: char *

Description: Pointer to PCX file.

Parameter: palette

Type: char *

Description: Location to store palette.

Comments: The function extracts the PCX format palette from a specified file and decodes it into a BIOS-compatible format. This buffer can then be used for making BIOS palette setting calls. Be sure the buffer palette is large enough to store all the palette information or your program may crash. Refer to gxGetDisplayPalette for buffer size requirements. The argument dType specifies the display type of the PCX file. Refer to gxSetDisplay for a listing of valid display types.

Return value: Success returns gxSUCCESS. Failure returns an error code (negative value).

See also: gxSetDisplay, gxGetDisplayPalette

Example:

```
/*-----------------------------------------------------------

Filename: pcxGFP.C

Function: pcxGetFilePalette

Description: Gets the color palette from the PCX file
            GENUS.PCX and prints the 16 colors
            in the palette
```

```
Prerequisite Function(s): gxSetDisplay
                          gxSetMode

See PrintError() function described in Appendix A

-------------------------------------------------------*/

#include <stdio.h>
#include <stdlib.h>
#include <conio.h>

#include <gxlib.h>
#include <pcxlib.h>

void PrintError(char * funcName, int retCode);

/* Global variables here... */

char * pcxFile = "Genus.PCX";
char palette[48];

void
main()
{
    int retValue;       /* Return value storage    */
    int dispMode;       /* 640x480x16 color        */
    int cnt;            /* Generic counter         */


    /* Local initialization section */

    dispMode = gxVGA_12; /* Set up 640x480x16 colors */
    retValue = 0;        /* Start clean              */

    /* Mandatory kernel initialization */

    retValue = gxSetDisplay(dispMode);
    if(retValue < 0)
    {
        PrintError("gxSetDisplay", retValue);
        return;
    }
```

```
/* Get the palette from the file */

retValue = pcxGetFilePalette(dispMode, pcxFile,
                             palette);
if(retValue < 0)
{
    PrintError("pcxGetFilePalette", retValue);
    return;
}

printf("The 16 RGB colors in the palette:\n");

for(cnt=0; cnt<48; cnt+=3)
    printf("R: %02d  G: %02d  B: %02d\n",
           palette[cnt], palette[cnt+1],
           palette[cnt+2]);

    return;
}
```

PCXGETFILETYPE

This function returns the display type of a specified PCX file.

Syntax: `int far pascal pcxGetFileType(fileName)`

Parameter: `fileName`

Type: `char *`

Description: Pointer to PCX file.

Comments: The function determines the display type of a PCX image file. This is the same type that is used for the `gxSetDisplay` calls. Occasionally, due to lack of header information, the function is unable to accurately determine the type. Note that the PowerPack only supports 2-color and 16-color image files, not 256-color.

Return value: Success returns `gxSUCCESS`. Failure returns an error code (negative value).

See also: `gxSetDisplay`, `gxGetDisplayPalette`

Example:

```
/*-----------------------------------------------------

Filename: pcxGFT.C

Function: pcxGetFileType

Description: Returns file type of GENUS.PCX

Prerequisite Function(s): gxSetDisplay
                          gxSetMode

See PrintError() function described in Appendix A

-----------------------------------------------------*/

#include <stdio.h>
#include <stdlib.h>
#include <conio.h>

#include <gxlib.h>
#include <pcxlib.h>

void PrintError(char * funcName, int retCode);

/* Global variables here... */

char * pcxFile = "Genus.PCX";

void
main()
{
    int retValue;       /* Return value storage    */
    int dispMode;       /* 640x480x16 color        */

    /* Local initialization section */

    dispMode = gxVGA_12; /* Set up 640x480x16 colors */
    retValue = 0;        /* Start clean              */

    /* Mandatory kernel initialization */

    retValue = gxSetDisplay(dispMode);
    if(retValue < 0)
    {
```

```
        PrintError("gxSetDisplay", retValue);
        return;
    }

    /* Get the file type information */

    retValue = pcxGetFileType(pcxFile);
    if(retValue < 0)
    {
        PrintError("pcxGetFileHeader", retValue);
        return;
    }

    /* Print the type */

    printf("%s File Type: %d\n",pcxFile,retValue);

    return;
}
```

PCXVERIFYFILE

This function verifies that a specified file is a valid PCX image file.

Syntax: int far pascal pcxVerifyFile(fileName)

Parameter: fileName

Type: char *

Description: Pointer to file.

Comments: Most of the PCX file functions automatically perform file type checking. This function enables you to access the file type checking routine.

Return value: Success returns gxSUCCESS if it is a valid PCX file. Failure returns an error code (negative value).

See also: pcxFileImage

Example:

```
/*-----------------------------------------------------------

Filename: pcxVF.C

Function: pcxVerifyFile

Description: Checks to see whether GENUS.PCX is a valid
             PCX file

Prerequisite Function(s): gxSetDisplay
                          gxSetMode

See PrintError() function described in Appendix A

-----------------------------------------------------------*/

#include <stdio.h>
#include <stdlib.h>
#include <conio.h>

#include <gxlib.h>
#include <pcxlib.h>

void PrintError(char * funcName, int retCode);

/* Global variables here... */

char * pcxFile = "Genus.PCX";
GXHEADER vHeader;

void
main()
{
    int retValue;          /* Return value storage    */
    int dispMode;          /* 640x480x16 color        */

    /* Local initialization section */

    dispMode = gxVGA_12; /* Set up 640x480x16 color   */
    retValue = 0;          /* Start clean              */

    /* Mandatory kernel initialization */
```

```
retValue = gxSetDisplay(dispMode);
if(retValue < 0)
{
    PrintError("gxSetDisplay", retValue);
    return;
}

/* Verify this is a PCX file */

retValue = pcxVerifyFile(pcxFile);
if(retValue == gxSUCCESS)
    printf("Yes, %s is a valid PCX file!\n
            ",pcxFile);
else
    PrintError("pcxVerifyFile", retValue);

return;
}
```

DATA STRUCTURE AND CONSTANT DEFINITIONS

GRAPHICS KERNEL ERROR CODES

```
#define gxSUCCESS        0    /* Successful */
#define gxERR_OPEN      -1    /* Error opening file */
#define gxERR_BUFSMALL  -2    /* Buffer is too small */
#define gxERR_READ      -3    /* Error in reading from
                                 file */
#define gxERR_WRITE     -4    /* Error in writing to
                                 file */
#define gxERR_BADDISP   -6    /* Display not defined/
                                 invalid */
#define gxERR_BADMODE   -7    /* Bad display mode */
```

```
#define gxERR_BADPAGE     -8    /* Bad page */
#define gxERR_BADPAL      -9    /* Bad palette  */
#define gxERR_NOPAL       -10   /* No palette available */
#define gxERR_NOTFOUND    -14   /* Image not found */
#define gxERR_BADMEMTYPE  -24   /* Bad virtual memory type */
#define gxERR_CMMFAIL     -25   /* General CMM alloc/free
                                   error */
#define gxERR_CMMNOMEM    -26   /* No CMM memory available */
#define gxERR_BADCOORD    -27   /* Bad coordinate location */
#define gxERR_NOTGX       -28   /* Not a valid gx buffer/
                                   file */
#define gxERR_CLOSE       -33   /* Error closing file */
#define gxERR_EOF         -35   /* End of file found */
#define gxERR_NOTIMPL     -900  /* Not implemented yet */
#define gxERR_GENERAL     -999  /* General error */
```

MAJOR GRAPHICS FUNCTIONS ERROR CODES

```
#define grSUCCESS          0    /* Successful */
#define grERR_BADFONT     -4000 /* Bad font type */
#define grERR_BADFILL     -4001 /* Bad fill style */
#define grERR_NODRIVER    -4002 /* No mouse driver found */
#define grERR_NOMOUSE     -4003 /* No mouse found */
#define grERR_BADCURSOR   -4004 /* Bad cursor style */
```

GRAPHICS EFFECTS FUNCTIONS ERROR CODES

```
#define fxSUCCESS          0    /* Successful */
#define fxERR_BADEFFECT   -2000 /* Effect not defined/
                                   invalid */
#define fxERR_BADGRAIN    -2001 /* Grain not defined/
                                   invalid */
#define fxERR_BADDELAY    -2002 /* Delay not defined/
                                   invalid */
#define fxERR_BADSIZE     -2003 /* Size of image masks
                                   invalid */
#define fxERR_NOSOUND     -2006 /* Sound card/driver not
                                   found */
#define fxERR_BADSOUND    -2012 /* Bad device/format/
                                   feature */
#define fxERR_NOTSOUND    -2013 /* Not a sound header */
#define fxERR_NOTSNG      -2014 /* Not a SNG file/
                                   buffer */
#define fxERR_DORMANT     -2018 /* Sound I/O is dormant */
#define fxERR_ACTIVE      -2019 /* Sound I/O is active */
```

PCX File Functions Error Codes

```
#define pcxSUCCESS        0      /* Successful */
#define pcxERR_NOTPCX    -3000  /* Not a valid pcx
                                    buffer/file */
```

Display Type Definitions

```
#define gxEGA_D    0    /* EGA Mode   DH ( 320x200x16 )*/
#define gxEGA_E    1    /* EGA Mode   EH ( 640x200x16 )*/
#define gxEGA_F    2    /* EGA Mode   FH ( 640x350x2  )*/
#define gxEGA_10   3    /* EGA Mode  10H ( 640x350x16 )*/
#define gxVGA_11   4    /* VGA Mode  11H ( 640x480x2  )*/
#define gxVGA_12   5    /* VGA Mode  12H ( 640x480x16 )*/
```

Graphics Kernel Colors

```
#define gxBLACK          0    /* Black         = 00H */
#define gxBLUE           1    /* Blue          = 01H */
#define gxGREEN          2    /* Green         = 02H */
#define gxCYAN           3    /* Cyan          = 03H */
#define gxRED            4    /* Red           = 04H */
#define gxMAGENTA        5    /* Magenta       = 05H */
#define gxBROWN          6    /* Brown         = 06H */
#define gxGRAY           7    /* Light Gray    = 07H */
#define gxDARKGRAY       8    /* Dark Gray     = 038H*/
#define gxLIGHTBLUE      9    /* Light Blue    = 039H*/
#define gxLIGHTGREEN    10    /* Light Green   = 03AH*/
#define gxLIGHTCYAN     11    /* Light Cyan    = 03BH*/
#define gxLIGHTRED      12    /* Light Red     = 03CH*/
#define gxLIGHTMAGENTA  13    /* Light Magenta= 03DH*/
#define gxYELLOW        14    /* Yellow        = 03EH*/
#define gxWHITE         15    /* White         = 03FH*/
```

Graphical Effects Types

```
#define fxMINEFFECT     0
#define fxBLIND         0    /* Blind */
#define fxCRUSH         1    /* Crush */
#define fxDIAGONAL      2    /* Diagonal */
#define fxDRIP          3    /* Drip */
#define fxEXPLODE       4    /* Explode */
#define fxRANDOM        5    /* Random */
```

```
#define fxSAND          6       /* Sand */
#define fxSLIDE         7       /* Slide */
#define fxSPIRAL        8       /* Spiral */
#define fxSPLIT         9       /* Split */
#define fxWEAVE         10      /* Weave */
#define fxWIPE          11      /* Wipe */
#define fxMAXEFFECT     11
```

GXDINFO STRUCTURE DEFINITION

```
typedef struct gxdinfo {
    char       dtype;       /* Display type */
    char       descrip[21]; /* String description */
    char       mode;        /* Actual BIOS mode */
    char       bitpx;       /* Number of bits per
                               pixel */
    unsigned   hres;        /* Horizontal resolution */
    unsigned   vres;        /* Vertical resolution */
    unsigned   bplin;       /* Number of bytes per
                               row */
    char       planes;      /* Number of display
                               planes */
    char       pages;       /* Number of display
                               pages */
    unsigned   begseg;      /* Beginning display
                               segment */
    unsigned   pagesize;    /* Size of display page */
    unsigned   paltype;     /* Palette format type */
} GXDINFO;

typedef GXDINFO far * GXDINFOPTR;
```

GXHEADER STRUCTURE DEFINITION

```
typedef struct gxheader {
    unsigned   id;          /* Virtual header ID
                               (=0CA00H) */
    unsigned   version;     /* Version number  */
    int        dtype;       /* Display type */
    unsigned   x1;          /* Picture dimensions
                               (incl) */
    unsigned   y1;
    unsigned   x2;
    unsigned   y2;
```

```
unsigned      hres;           /* Display horizontal
                                 resolution */
unsigned      vres;           /* Display vertical
                                 resolution */
char          nplanes;        /* Number of planes */
char          bitpx;          /* Bits per pixel */
unsigned      bplin;          /* Bytes per line */
unsigned      vtype;          /* Virtual buffer type */
char far *    vptr;           /* Virtual buffer
                                 pointer */
unsigned      ptype;          /* Palette type */
char far *    pptr;           /* Palette buffer
                                 pointer */
char          reserved[94];   /* Reserved for GX
                                 kernel */
} GXHEADER;

typedef GXHEADER far * GXHEADERPTR;
```

PCXHEADER STRUCTURE DEFINITION

```
typedef struct pcxheader {
    char          manuf;          /* Always =10 for Paint
                                     brush */
    char          hard;           /* Version information */
    char          encod;          /* Run-length encoding
                                     (=1) */
    char          bitpx;          /* Bits per pixel */
    unsigned      x1;             /* Picture dimensions
                                     (incl) */
    unsigned      y1;
    unsigned      x2;
    unsigned      y2;
    unsigned      hres;           /* Horizontal DPI
                                     resolution */
    unsigned      vres;           /* Vertical DPI
                                     resolution */
    char          clrma[48];      /* Palette */
    char          vmode;          /* (ignored) */
    char          nplanes;        /* Number of planes (ver
                                     2.5=0) */
    unsigned      bplin;          /* Bytes per line */
    unsigned      palinfo;        /* Palette Info (1=col,
                                     2=gray) */
```

```
        unsigned     shres;        /* Horiz display
                                      resolution  */
        unsigned     svres;        /* Vert display
                                      resolution */
        char         xtra[54];     /* Extra space (filler) */
} PCXHEADER;

typedef PCXHEADER     *PCXHEADERPTR;
```

GRSTATE STRUCTURE DEFINITION

```
typedef struct grstate {
        int          page;      /* Page */
        int          pageofs;   /* Page offset */
        int          color;     /* Foreground color */
        int          bkcolor;   /* Background color */
        int          firstpt;   /* First point plot flag */
        int          cpx;       /* Current position (x,y) */
        int          cpy;       /* */
        int          op;        /* Logical operation */
        int          clip;      /* Clipping flag */
        int          clipx1;    /* Clipping region: (x1,y1) */
        int          clipy1;    /* */
        int          clipx2;    /* to  (x2,y2)       */
        int          clipy2;    /* */
        int          fstyle;    /* Fill style */
        int          fcolor;    /* Fill color */
        int          ftrans;    /* Fill transparency */
        int          lstyle;    /* Line style */
        int          lthick;    /* Line thickness */
        int          viewrox;   /* Viewport origin: (ox,oy) */
        int          viewroy;   /*(relative to viewport) */
        int          viewx1;    /* Viewport region: (x1,y1) */
        int          viewy1;    /* */
        int          viewx2;    /* to  (x2,y2) */
        int          viewy2;    /* */
        int          tstyle;    /* Text style */
        int          ttrans;    /* Text transparency */
        int          thjust;    /* Text justification */
        int          tvjust;    /* */
} GRSTATE;

typedef GRSTATE far * GRSTATEPTR;
```

FILL PATTERN STYLES

```
#define grFMIN        0     /* Minimum fill */
#define grFSOLID      0     /* Solid */
#define grFLINE       1     /* Horizontal lines === */
#define grFSLASH      2     /* Forward slashes /// */
#define grFTHSLASH    3     /* Thick forward slashes ///*/
#define grFBKSLASH    4     /* Backward slashes \\\ */
#define grFTHBKSLASH  5     /* Thick backward slashes \\\*/
#define grFHATCH      6     /* Crosshatch XXX */
#define grFTHHATCH    7     /* Thick crosshatch XXX */
#define grFINTER      8     /* Interleaved lines +++ */
#define grFWIDEDOT    9     /* Wide spaced dots ... */
#define grFCLOSEDOT   10    /* Close spaced dots ::: */
#define grFUSER       11    /* User-defined ??? */
#define grFMAX        11    /* Maximum fill */
```

LINE STYLES

```
#define grLSOLID     0xFFFF  /* Solid _____ */
#define grLHUGEDASH  0xFFF0  /* Huge dashes _____ ___ */
#define grLBIGDASH   0xFF00  /* Big dashes ____    ____ */
#define grLMEDDASH   0xF0F0  /* Medium dashes __   ____   */
#define grLSMALLDASH 0xCCCC  /* Small dashes __ __ __ __ */
#define grLWIDEDOT   0x8888  /* Wide dots . . . . . . */
#define grLCLOSEDOT  0xAAAA  /* Close dots ............ */
#define grLDASHDOT   0xFAFA  /* Dash dot __.__.__.__. */
#define grLCENTER    0xFDBF  /* Center line ____ . ____ */
```

MUSIC DEFINITION LANGUAGE

Command Type	Command	Description
Selecting an Octave	O*n*	Sets the current octave to *n*, where *n* can range from 0–9.
	>	Increases current octave by 1. If current octave is 9, this has no effect.
	<	Decreases current octave by 1. If current octave is 0, this has no effect.

continues

Command Type	Command	Description
Selecting a Note	A–G	Plays the notes A–G in current octave and length.
	N*nn*	Plays the note *nn*. There are 10 octaves with 12 notes per octave, so *nn* can range from 1–120. A value of 0 specifies a rest.
	# or +	Placed after a note, this specifies a sharp (as in C#).
	–	Placed after a note, this specifies a flat (as in D–).
Selecting a Length	L*nn*	Selects the default note length, as 1/*nn*. Therefore, *nn*=1 is a whole note, *nn*=2 is a half note, *nn*=4 is a quarter note, and so on. The range for *nn* is 1–64. The note length also can be given immediately after the note, as C4 (which is equivalent to L4 C).
	.	A period placed after a note causes that note to play 3/2 its originally specified length.
	MS	Music Staccato. Each note plays 3/4 of the length specified by L.
	MN	Music Normal. Each note plays 7/8 of the length specified by L.
	ML	Music Legato. Each note plays the full length specified by L.
Selecting a Tempo	T*nn*	Specifies the number of 1/4 notes in a minute. The tempo defaults to 120 with a range of 30–255.

Command Type	Command	Description
	P*nn*	Specifies a Pause, with *nn* specifying the pause length.
Selecting Background	MF	Music Foreground. The entire string is played before control is returned to the program. This is the default.
	MB	Music Background. The entire string is placed into a buffer first; then control is returned to the program. The background buffer is limited to 128 notes.

PrintError Source Code

```
/*-----------------------------------------------------

Filename: prERROR.C

Function: PrintError

Description: This function prints a meaningful error
            message whenever one of the functions fail.
            This function is required by all of the
            example programs.

Prerequisite Function(s): none

-----------------------------------------------------*/

#include <stdio.h>
#include <stdlib.h>
#include <dos.h>

#include <gxlib.h>
#include <grlib.h>
#include <fxlib.h>
#include <pcxlib.h>
```

```
void
PrintError(char * fName, int retVal)
{

  printf("The function \"%s\" returned ", fName);

  switch(retVal){

    case gxERR_OPEN:
      printf("gxERR_OPEN - Error opening file.");
      break;
    case gxERR_BUFSMALL:
      printf("gxERR_BUFSMALL - Buffer too small.");
      break;
    case gxERR_READ:
      printf("gxERR_READ - Error reading from file.");
      break;
    case gxERR_WRITE:
      printf("gxERR_WRITE - Error writing to file.");
      break;
    case gxERR_BADDISP:
      printf("gxERR_BADDISP - Invalid display type.");
      break;
    case gxERR_BADMODE:
      printf("gxERR_BADMODE - Bad video mode.");
      break;
    case gxERR_BADPAGE:
      printf("gxERR_BADPAGE - Bad page number.");
      break;
    case gxERR_BADPAL:
      printf("gxERR_BADPAL - Bad palette.");
      break;
    case gxERR_NOPAL:
      printf("gxERR_NOPAL - No palette available.");
      break;
    case gxERR_NOTFOUND:
      printf("gxERR_NOTFOUND - Image not found.");
      break;
    case gxERR_BADMEMTYPE:
      printf("gxERR_BADMEMTYPE - Bad virtual memory type.");
      break;
    case gxERR_CMMFAIL:
      printf("gxERR_CMMFAIL - CMM Alloc/dealloc failure.");
      break;
    case gxERR_CMMNOMEM:
      printf("gxERR_CMMNOMEM - Not enough CMM memory.");
      break;
```

```
case gxERR_BADCOORD:
  printf("gxERR_BADCOORD - Bad pixel coordinate.");
  break;
case gxERR_NOTGX:
  printf("gxERR_NOTGX - Not a GX compatible file.");
  break;
case gxERR_CLOSE:
  printf("gxERR_CLOSE - Error closing file.");
  break;
case gxERR_EOF:
  printf("gxERR_EOF - Unexpected End Of File.");
  break;
case gxERR_NOTIMPL:
  printf("gxERR_NOTIMPL - Function not implemented.");
  break;
case gxERR_GENERAL:
  printf("gxERR_GENERAL - General function failure.");
  break;
case grERR_BADFONT:
  printf("grERR_BADFONT - Bad font style.");
  break;
case grERR_BADFILL:
  printf("grERR_BADFILL - Bad fill style.");
  break;
case grERR_BADCURSOR:
  printf("grERR_BADCURSOR - Bad cursor style.");
  break;
case fxERR_BADEFFECT:
  printf("fxERR_BADEFFECT - Bad effect type.");
  break;
case fxERR_BADGRAIN:
  printf("fxERR_BADGRAIN - Bad grain size.");
  break;
case fxERR_BADDELAY:
  printf("fxERR_BADDELAY - Bad delay size.");
  break;
case fxERR_BADSIZE:
  printf("fxERR_BADSIZE - Bad size.");
  break;
case fxERR_NOSOUND:
  printf("fxERR_NOSOUND - No sound driver installed.");
  break;
case fxERR_BADSOUND:
  printf("fxERR_BADSOUND - Bad sound type.");
  break;
```

```
      case fxERR_NOTSOUND:
        printf("fxERR_NOTSOUND - Not a sound buffer.");
        break;
      case fxERR_NOTSNG:
        printf("fxERR_NOTSNG - Not a song buffer.");
        break;
      case fxERR_DORMANT:
        printf("fxERR_DORMANT - Sound is currently dormant.");
        break;
      case fxERR_ACTIVE:
        printf("fxERR_ACTIVE - Sound is currently active.");
        break;
      case pcxERR_NOTPCX:
        printf("pcxERR_NOTPCX - Not a PCX file.");
        break;
      default:
        printf("%d. Check the PowerPack Appendix.\n",retValue);
        break;
  }

  putchar('\n');

}
```

THE APPLES &
ORANGES GAME

The Apples & Oranges game is on the disk included with this book. Apples & Oranges is a two-player game in which each player is represented by an apple or an orange. You can also play against the computer. Each player tries to capture the most pieces on the board by surrounding the other player's pieces. An opponent's pieces are surrounded when a player's piece exists on both ends of a straight line. After a move is made, all surrounded pieces in all directions (including diagonally) are flipped to the moving player's piece. The game ends when no valid moves can be made, and the winner is the player with the most pieces. The game requires at least an EGA adapter and monitor, and a mouse.

To begin the game, simply change to the directory where you installed the game and type **A&O** at the DOS prompt. The executable is installed with the installation program.

APPLES & ORANGES OPTIONS

To change the playing level, simply click the LEVEL button to cycle through the level options. For computer play, select playing Level 1, 2, or 3. Otherwise, select the two-player option. The computer uses a different algorithm on each level when it is playing, with Level 3 as the most difficult.

The active player is indicated by the beveled buttons at the right edge of the screen. An UP button indicates the current player's turn. In addition, the mouse cursor identifies the current player's valid moves when placed over the board.

Select the NEW option at any time to reset the current board to the initial, four-piece board. It does not ask you if you are sure, so do not select it unless you mean it.

If you make a move accidentally, or you just want to change it, select the UNDO button. In two-player mode, it will undo the last player's move only. When playing the computer, it will undo your move, and the last computer move. Selecting UNDO twice will undo the undo, which restores the board to its original state.

To get a hint on your next move, select the HINT button. The computer uses the best algorithm, and then flashes the place it recommends you move to. If you select HINT several times, without making a move, you may notice it does not necessarily recommend the same place every time. This occurs when several moves have the same weighted score.

Help is available by selecting the RULES button. A pop-up window is displayed, with a summary of the game play and rules. Click the mouse or press a key to remove the help window.

To end the game and exit back to DOS, select the QUIT button. You are immediately returned to DOS, regardless of the status of the current game.

MAKING A MOVE

A player can move only in places that capture at least one of the opponent's pieces. If a move is valid, the cursor changes to the current player's symbol (Apple or Orange). If a player can make no valid moves, the turn is automatically forfeited.

A player makes a move by positioning the mouse cursor over the board. Click the left mouse button to make a move. All captured pieces are then pushed, flipped, and counted in all directions.

The winner is determined once all valid moves have been made, or there are no more squares on the board. The player with the most pieces is declared the winner.

PROGRAMMING

A&O uses many of the features of the Graphics PowerPack:

GX Kernel: Hardware detection and verification; display and mode setting; virtual buffer creation, manipulation, and display; buffer optimization; timing; and random numbers.

GX Graphics: Keyboard and mouse interfacing; custom mouse cursors; dynamic cursor types; efficient mouse click decoding; pop-up windows; text, line, and fill styles; and drawing.

GX Effects: PC Speaker background music; and special effects.

PCX Toolkit: Loading PCX images.

TECHNIQUES

In addition to the Graphics PowerPack implementation, A&O illustrates some common gaming techniques. The first is the use of the board algorithm. This algorithm is used when playing the game against the computer, to give the computer its Thinking capability. The first level is totally random, and it can do a pretty good job of keeping up with you. The second level would seem to be the best, for it looks for the maximum pieces it can flip. After all, that's what most players do when playing the game. The third level uses a weighted algorithm to play the game, and does not look at the pieces flipped at all. It knows that by capturing the corners, the player will eventually be able to flip more pieces. There is room for improvement, however, as detailed later.

The board layout is another demonstrated gaming technique. It has a lot to do with mouse input and decoding. The A&O board has 64 squares, which would take forever to test individually, and would create unnecessary code. Instead, the entire board is treated as a mouse click region. If a click is detected inside the board, it is not tested against each button position, but is decoded by columns and rows. This helps for the valid position cursor logic.

The valid move logic has been optimized to search for only the first valid move—not all valid moves. By breaking up the function this way, a valid move is checked individually or in groups. Because the move logic is constantly checked against the cursor position, it is important that this be done quickly.

Even the video mode has been selected in order to be compatible with a wider range of systems. The game requires only an EGA adapter and display, which is technology that has been available for over five years.

SUGGESTIONS FOR IMPROVEMENT

The following suggestions are ideas for program enhancement or improvement. Implementing some of these features is an excellent way to learn more about the Graphics PowerPack—and they're fun!

Modify Tie. By default, a tie goes to the ORANGE player. This is not exactly fair. Modify the CheckWin function so that it displays a "Tie" message. For an effect, draw a Banana image the same size as the Apple and Orange playing pieces—and use the same display logic to fade it to the screen.

Piece Flips. When an Apple captures an Orange, or vice versa, use an animation sequence. You can make the pieces look like they are being flipped. Draw three views of each piece getting thinner. If an Apple takes an Orange, show the Orange getting thinner, then the Apple getting thicker. This gives the illusion that the piece is being flipped like a coin.

New Levels. The board algorithms for the computer are very straightforward. Add a Level 4 that combines Levels 2 and 3. This means that if more than one move exists with the same board weight, you can see which move flips the most pieces (instead of selecting one randomly). For Level 5, add a look-ahead feature. You can look not only at the computer's best move, but ahead to what is the best responding move. Does the computer's move allow the player to capture most of the pieces back?

Index

ADD THE POWER OF GRAPHICS
TO YOUR PROGRAMS WITH GENUS

PCX TOOLKIT 5.0   *NEW!*

The number one PCX toolkit is now better than ever! With the PCX Toolkit, you can incorporate graphics into your programs quickly and easily. The PCX Toolkit includes over 90 routines to display, save, scale, and manipulate PCX bitmapped graphics from almost any program.

. . . . ONLY $249

GX EFFECTS 2.0*

Add spectacular special effects (F/X) to your programs, without being trapped in someone else's editor or slideshow program. Wipe, split, crush, slide, sand, drip, diagonal, spiral, random, or explode your graphics. Includes new animation support and sprite capabilities.

. . . . ONLY $199

* PCX Toolkit, GX Graphics, or GX Text recommended but not required.

GX TEXT 2.0

Now you can display blazing bitmapped text in any graphics mode as simply as text mode. With GX Text, you can display your textual information right along with your graphical data, using the display or virtual buffers. Includes a graphical font editor and 1MB+ of fonts.

. . . . ONLY $149

GX GRAPHICS 2.0   *NEW!*

A complete graphics library supporting all graphics primitives. Use the GX Graphics toolkit instead of the BGI or MS libraries and make your program faster, smaller, and more portable across compilers – while supporting more video modes.

. . . . ONLY $199

ALSO AVAILABLE: GX GAMES . . . . ONLY $59

Although many personal computers use 3 1/2-inch disks to store information, some older computers use 5 1/4-inch disks for information storage. If your computer uses 5 1/4-inch disks, you can return this form to Sams Publishing to obtain 5 1/4-inch disks to use with this book. Complete the remainder of this form and mail to

Graphics Programming PowerPack,
First Edition
Disk Exchange
Sams Publishing
11711 N. College Ave., Suite 140
Carmel, IN 46032

We will send you, free of charge, the 5 1/4-inch version of the book software.

Name_____Phone_____

Company_____Title_____

Address _____

City_____State____ZIP_____

INSTALLING THE DISK

To install the PowerPack on your computer system, place the PowerPack disk in drive A: and enter the following two lines (if you are installing from another drive, substitute that letter for the A:):

```
A:
INSTALL
```

Follow the menu options for installing various parts of the PowerPack, using the directories you wish. All programs and files are verified for data integrity, to ensure nothing is lost in the installation process. No modifications are performed on your environment (that is, your AUTOEXEC.BAT and CONFIG.SYS files). You can run the installation program more than once, if you later wish to install parts of the PowerPack you decide to skip now.

WHAT'S ON THE GRAPHICS PROGRAMMING POWERPACK DISK?

The Graphics Programming PowerPack is a collection of functions from the GX Development Series by Genus Microprogramming, Inc. The GX Development Series is an extremely powerful, flexible, yet easy-to-use graphics toolkit package, hand-coded and optimized in assembly language for maximum speed. The PowerPack disk was created by selecting the most useful routines from the GX Development Series toolkit packages and putting them together in one toolkit included with this book.

The PowerPack disk consists of a DOS Link Library and sample source code. The aim of this library is to accelerate and simplify graphics application building under DOS. The libraries, include files, and examples are provided on the disk.

The PowerPack is separated into four distinct graphics groups. Each group contains a unique header file and link library for small, medium, and large memory models. The following list is a detailed description of these groups.

1. **Kernel**: The kernel provides the very basic graphics functionality and is the heart of the PowerPack. The kernel contains basic functions such as gxSetMode (set the current display mode) and gxClearDisplay (clear a display page).

2. **Graphics Routines**: The graphics routines are a supplement to the kernel, providing the vast majority of graphics operations such as grSetFillPattern (select a fill pattern) and grDrawRect (draw a rectangle).

3. **Effects Routines**: The effects routines contain functions specific to special effects, such as fxPlaySong (play a string of notes) and fxPlayTone (play a frequency tone).

4. **PCX Routines**: The PCX routines contain functions that allow the display of PCX files such as pcxVerifyFile (verify if valid PCX file) and pcxFileImage (load PCX file into memory).

5. **Apples & Oranges**: As an extra bonus, the PowerPack includes the Apples & Oranges game, called A&O. The full source code is provided, along with the necessary image files.